AF469762

THE
NEW
FOREST
900 YEARS AFTER

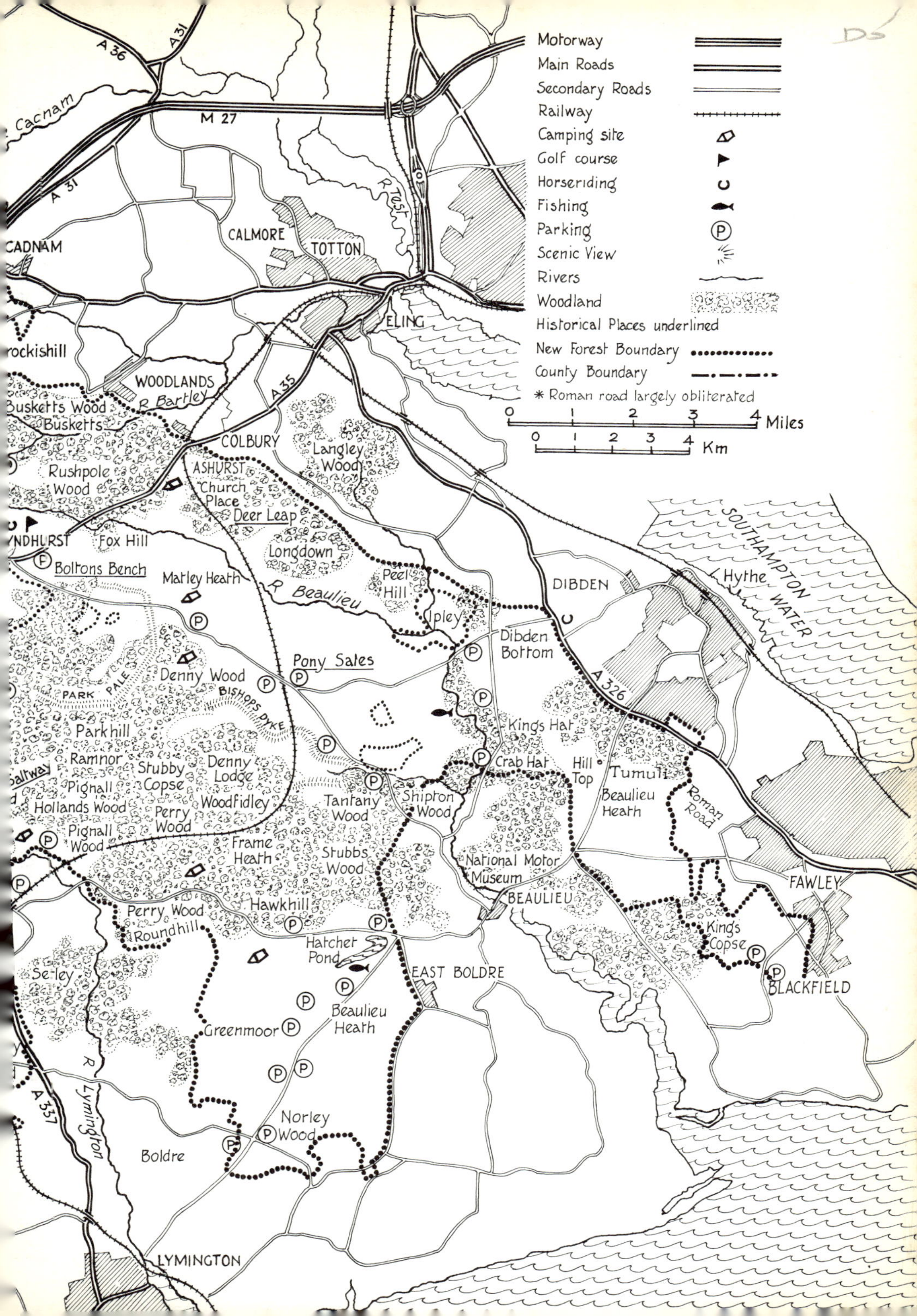

Motorway
Main Roads
Secondary Roads
Railway
Camping site
Golf course
Horseriding
Fishing
Parking
Scenic View
Rivers
Woodland
Historical Places underlined
New Forest Boundary
County Boundary
* Roman road largely obliterated
0 1 2 3 4 Miles
0 1 2 3 4 Km
A 36
A 31
M 27
A 31
Cacnam
CADNAM
CALMORE
TOTTON
R Test
ELING
rockishill
WOODLANDS
R Bartley
A 35
Busketts Wood
Busketts
COLBURY
Langley Wood
Rushpole Wood
ASHURST
Church Place
Deer Leap
YNDHURST
Fox Hill
Longdown
Boltons Bench
Matley Heath
R Beaulieu
Peel Hill
DIBDEN
Hythe
SOUTHAMPTON WATER
Ipley
Dibden Bottom
Pony Sales
A 326
Denny Wood
PARK PALE
BISHOPS DYKE
Parkhill
Kings Hat
Ramnor
Stubby Copse
Denny Lodge
Crab Hat
Hill Top
Tumuli
Roman Road
Pignall
Hollands Wood
Perry Wood
Woodfidley
Tantany Wood
Shipton Wood
Beaulieu Heath
Pignall Wood
Frame Heath
Stubbs Wood
National Motor Museum
FAWLEY
BEAULIEU
Perry Wood
Roundhill
Hawkhill
Kings Copse
Hatchet Pond
EAST BOLDRE
BLACKFIELD
Setley
Greenmoor
Beaulieu Heath
R Lymington
A 337
Norley Wood
Boldre
LYMINGTON

PETER TATE

MACDONALD AND JANE'S · LONDON

Dedication

For Lesley and Mark,
my good companions

A Raven Book
This is a joint project of
Macdonald and Jane's Publishers Limited
and Futura Publications Limited

First published in Great Britain in 1979 by
Macdonald and Jane's Publishers Limited
Paulton House
8 Shepherdess Walk
London N1 7LW

ISBN 0 354 04362 5

Filmset in 'Monophoto' Plantin by
Servis Filmsetting Limited, Manchester

Printed and bound in Great Britain by
Purnell and Sons Limited
Paulton, Bristol

Contents

ILLUSTRATIONS

My grateful thanks are due to:
SIMON ROWLEY for the pictures on pages 16, 43, 46, 57, 60, 70, 77, 99, 107, 132, 136, 145, 152, 153.
HARRY W. ASHLEY for the jacket illustration and the pictures on pages 63, 67, 95, 111, 163, 164, 169; Mr Ashley and the *Evening Echo*, Bournemouth for illustrations on pages 24, 163.
GORDON JONES and *Evening Echo*, Bournemouth for photographs on pages 21, 79.
SOUTHERN NEWSPAPERS LTD for the picture on page 82.
SOUTHERN TELEVISION LTD for the picture on page 55.
E.V. LEYDEN for the picture on page 90.
PRESS ASSOCIATION for pictures on pages 102, 172.
KEN HOSKIN of J.W. Kitchenham Ltd for the picture on page 138.

Drawings for chapter headings were done by Corinne Burrows.

My thanks are due to all who have spared me their time, their tolerance and their experience in this project, but particularly to: Sir Dudley Forwood, Bt., Official Verderer; Mr David Stagg, member of the New Forest Association; Mr Donn Small, Deputy Surveyor, and Forestry Commission staff; Mr Colin Tubbs of the Nature Conservancy; all of whom provided information without which this work would lack authority; Miss Angela Milne for her help in the preparation of the manuscript and Mr A. Spark whose map pinpoints my wanderings. Also all those ordinary people who have opened their mouths, their hearts and their homes to me during those wanderings.

Peter Tate

Perambulation

IT has been another day of wide-eyed discovery in the New Forest. This morning, we found an oakwood on Lyndhurst Hill where the grey squirrels were so plentiful that we could not turn in any direction without seeing at least two more of the bannertail brethren. This afternoon, at Bisterne Closes, though the calendar said June, we walked on a constant autumn of beechmast among smooth grey-green trunks that had escaped the axe but not, sadly, the pen-knife.

In 1079, on such a day, perhaps with just such a tinge of concern, William the Conqueror considered the 200 square miles of furzy waste and well-established woodland which lay in the dip of the Hampshire Basin, bounded in the east by Southampton Water and in the west by the River Avon, in the north by the chalk downlands and in the south by the sea. This was Ytene (rhymes with 'Brittany'), as the Saxons called it, translatable as 'furzy waste' and 'land of the Jutes'.

No doubt he saw a favourite hunting ground, but my feeling is that he observed a great deal more. A king who 'loved the great deer as their father' was not solely occupied with the chase or the banqueting table.

In a horseback tour of no great distance or duration, he could well have come across abandoned pottery sites around Sloden with the upturned clay still lying as raw and red as at the potters' Bronze Age beginnings. At Matley, between the villages of Lyndhurst and Brockenhurst (Linhest and Brokenhest, as they were at Domesday), perhaps good grazing land had been peeled away by the turf cutters to warm their hearths. In Bolderwood, there were charcoal-burners and they could have been over-zealous. Or did the irritation come from too many tree-wounds weeping sap because impatient peasants wanted their firewood before it touched the ground?

Whatever he saw, this unschooled Norman had reason enough to safeguard a unique overlap of environment. Nine centuries on, when we claim to understand so much more of the meaning of conservation, we should still be rejoicing that William took that first vital step.

I am grateful: hence this book. And if, by reading it, you can come to share with me in joy, then I will feel I am taking something off a debt that has been outstanding for close on a thousand years.

Actually, that makes the mission sound rather formal and serious, when all I can really do is to try and communicate the kind of quiet excitement which takes me whenever the cool, green branches close over my head.

The oak's gnarls mean experience, the beech's smooth stalk is strength and purpose. These trees are older than I am and I can't help feeling that makes them wiser.

The conifers do not instil the same confidence. These plantations were begun a mere 200 years ago, which, in tree terms, is almost my generation. They live one-third as long and three times as fast as the broadleaves. They were introduced to make money, and although their pedigree is every bit as impeccable the fact gives them a kind of shiftiness for me. They may have brought the rhododendrons and the breeding crossbill as bright accompaniments to their tenure, but I am still not convinced. I don't trust the darkness under their woven fingers and the unseasonal chill of it makes me shiver.

I could put that into official language, and tell you that by preferring oaks and beeches to conifers I am favouring the Ancient and Ornamental Woodlands (which, with the Open Forest Waste of heath, bog and emergent woodland, total 65,000 acres) to the 18,000-plus acres of Statutory Timber Inclosures; that New Forest broadleaves produce a naturally regenerated successor crop and renew themselves at the rate of approximately 12 acres a year; with much more besides. But just now I would rather go on to something no official survey would mention – the effect, in the Forest, of the weather.

For a grey sky is as important to moorland nuances as the sun is to the seaside. Only under leaden and towering cumulus does the bell-heather proffer its full vivacity, or the wild rhododendron its fuchsia glow, or the gorse its flickering warmth. And it is a mark of the Forest that poor weather can be offset by endearing behaviour or an unexpected glimpse of beauty. The way clouds will clear to present you with a spectacular end to an unspectacular day can only be described as apologetic.

We saw this for ourselves one day at Easter, 1975, when we were on our way home to South Wales, having spent a week looking at the houses we liked in the Forest area and about half a day viewing the ones we could afford. To prime us for the journey, we – that is, my wife Lesley, teenaged son Mark and I – decided to follow the ornamental drive through Knightwood, Mark Ash and Bolderwood before we took the A31 westward to Ringwood and then branched north through Verwood and on to our usual route over Cranborne Chase.

The weather during the whole week had been eccentric. Two days earlier, we had walked along the seafront from Alum Chine to Sandbanks and had to stop at the 'crystal palace' which serves as the Branksome Chine cafe for a drink to cool us from the strong April sun. On the way back, an hour later, we had to stop there again after running the last 100 yards under a barrage of hail.

Even as we sat in the cafe, warming hands around cups, the hail turned to blizzard and we watched the peculiar effect of snow upon waterline. It was as though the tide was coming from inland, so that ebb and flow were marked with a Doppelganger dappling far whiter than any salt wash.

Now, we were driving up the A35 towards Lyndhurst when a black cloud of ogre-like aspect heaved itself up over Holidays Hill and waited above the Knightwood turn-off, almost daring us to enter.

Our thoughts were of thunder and particularly of lightning. But, half a mile short of Knightwood, soft white flakes began to pick at the windscreen. By the time we made our turn, we were immersed, involved, absorbed into the choreography of falling snow.

That would have been impressive enough, with the pines and uncurling ferns of Knightwood for a backdrop but, not fifty metres in from the main road, hugging the shelter which I have called chilling and unfriendly, were a court of fallow does, about eight or nine, some standing, some reclining. They regarded us squarely but made no show of anxiety beyond a flicker of an ear.

I shut off the engine and we returned their gaze, the one party most certainly enchanted, the other seemingly in no hurry to end the spell, and the snow fell between us and around us and made us, it seemed, all part of the same whitening tableau. We might have been fellow inhabitants of a toy glass sphere waiting for the whim of some giant handler to set the flakes swirling again.

When we felt we could trespass no more upon their privacy, we quietly

Snow in the Forest at Burley Lodge.

took our leave. The fall had stopped, in snow terms a mere pup. But the talcum layer upon Bolderwood and Verely gave us a strong hint of what the Forest could be like in the event of a real storm. (Like the winter of 1963, I was thinking, when 300 deer and ponies lay dead among trees bowed down by the weight of snow and sorrow.)

On another occasion, we had stalked the ancient capital of Winchester in the kind of rain that invariably sweeps cobbled streets and cathedral purlieu whenever we are in the vicinity. Downfalls there never bother us. They have the Florentine effect of producing cascades from the most unlikely sources and drawing your eyes to gutters and grotesques you would never notice in the dry.

And now, when we had returned to the Forest coastland at Milford, the sky decided to make its act of contrition. The drab cloud rolled away to the east like a blind lifted after mourning and at a comparable speed.

Dispel the thought that rainbows are for chasing but never for catching because here, upon the cliff-top, we stood beneath the centre of the arch. The bow, begun upon the ploughed farmlands of Hordle, dropped to its completion in the sea between us and the four-miles-distant Isle of Wight. If I could have reached out a cup, it would have come back brimming with spectral water.

It dissolved in this way, receding first from the sea and then, just when you thought the process would follow the line of the arch, developing a shimmer that took it all away in the blink of an eye. But the show was not over.

Michelangelo, given his way with a basilica ceiling, could not have matched this dome of sky. The full repertoire of cirrus and nimbus busied across it like acrobats, rolling, flowing, writhing, tyre-tracking, covering every shade from pale orange through to magenta. And the breezes which powered the action seemed no less versatile. Clouds moved on collision courses and then passed each other safely, above and below. Herringbone became pink horse and alto-cumulus flattened and thinned to herringbone.

This red sky at night might not prove to be a shepherd's delight but it was certainly ours while it lasted. Then the sun, doubtless tired by all this manipulation so late in the day, lowered itself quickly beyond Hengistbury and Purbeck and pulled down a final curtain of purple on the display.

I make no excuse for such anecdotes of personal experience, because anecdotes are what you will take home from the New Forest. They are cheap, do not break when you drop them and can be given to just about anybody. Furthermore, they will be unique because the same thing never happens to different people, nor twice to the same one. You will be ready to think old Ytene looks upon you with some special favour, which is true enough . . . except that he does it for everybody.

So this book does not fight shy of anecdotes. Indeed, the whole thing is, I hope, more of a personal experience than a guidebook. I have given it history, facts and figures, but in searching them out I have talked as well as travelled, because the New Forest does not live by trees alone but by men and women. My tour has had its moments of high drama; the result was far better than I would have dared to hope. So armed, I can tell you a great deal that you cannot have read elsewhere about this ancient tract of waste and woodland, about the people who run it and the creatures who enjoy it and the factors that make it unique. Put that alongside your own first-hand experience of the place and you will come to love and understand the Forest that conquered William.

Pledges and Peacocks

THE Official Verderer of the Forest, the man at the top, must surely be the first person we meet. History can wait while we make our visit to Sir Dudley Forwood, third Bt., aged 66, veteran of the diplomatic service, honorary director of Cruft's Dog Show, past director of the Royal Show, former Equerry to the Duke of Windsor, and resident at the Old House, which is actually almost a new house. (But in a New Forest which is a very old forest this somehow seems all right.)

The drive up to the house is more than one-and-a-half miles, starting with broadleaf and birch to the right and Norway spruce to the left and switching to total conifer after the first Forestry Commission ride crosses it. As grit roads go, there are few complaints, except of occasional narrowness and a tendency for the verges to drop away sharply in a manner that might catch a straying wheel.

Sir Dudley has a thick file of correspondence going back eight years to document this fact and confirm beyond any doubt that the road is not that good because it leads to the home of the Official Verderer. But then he happens to care about such things – and the worst any of his enemies in the Forest can find against him is that he is 'straight'. More than can be said for the drive, which swings this way and that before half-circling Sir Dudley's eleven acres to let you in across a cattle grid which bothers him because it is too shallow to keep the ponies away from his daffodils – enough daffodils to disable a Wordsworth.

If, with the car window rolled down as you listen for barks from the deer at Burley Lodge, you fancied you heard instead the heckling of peacocks, you would be right. In blue glory, they patrol his paths and play the gargoyle on his window ledges.

'A friend of my wife was looking for a home for one,' says Sir Dudley. 'My wife said, "For goodness' sake, don't mention it to Dudley." When the friend asked me, "Will you take it?" I said, "Yes – but for goodness' sake don't mention it to Mary."'

Either way, at the Old House, there are now at least 12 peacocks and peahens, including one white who has woman trouble – his senior wife keeps throwing the harem newcomer's eggs around the communal cage, or it may be the other way about. And each morning the uncaged blues rise to the upper storey to greet the sun – and none of the east-facing guest rooms needs an alarm clock.

The new Old House, with its Palladian bays and porches, looks older than the old Old House, which it replaced. It was set up in 1966 when, says Sir Dudley, 'you could build a decent house at a decent price.' The work became necessary because the premises where the Hon. Auberon Herbert had fed the gypsy children on strawberries and swung in his barber's chair, in his transparent tower, to view the Forest in all directions, were without proper plumbing and impossible to heat overall at one time.

The first architect Sir Dudley called in wanted to put the bedrooms on one side of the house and the bathrooms on the other. When Sir Dudley objected on the grounds of inconvenience, the expert declared himself thwarted and departed. The Forwoods then called in a young friend who had just failed his architect's examinations and the lines were drawn – to everybody's satisfaction.

The threshold, which looks genuine Regency enough to have had Prinny cross it, lets into a large hall furnished for living with sofas which almost swallow you, flowers, pictures, china dogs and horses. The wall panelling and the Adam staircase which leads to a balcony – as well as the Wedgwood plaques in the dining-room beyond – have come from New Park, Brockenhurst. 'John Morant was a good friend of mine,' says Sir Dudley. 'He let me have them very reasonably.'

He hesitates to use the word 'classical' but prefers the solid-sounding 'good' for this superior style of dwelling. He knows what he likes but refuses to make it sound pretentious.

The sherry is good, the portrait of Lady Forwood attended by King

Sir Dudley Forwood, Bt., Official Verderer, on his pure-bred Arab, Shamanto, leaves his home near Burley to join an agister in a welfare check on Forest animals.

Charles spaniels in a woodland setting is good, the feeling of the interview is . . . good.

Sir Dudley came to the Forest sixty years ago with his parents when his father retired from the shipping business in Liverpool. Though his services to diplomacy have taken him to many parts of the world since, he has spent enough time in Forest circles to be intimately involved with the horse and hunt sections of the community as well as the welfare and conservational interests embodied in his position as chief administrator of the Court of Verderers.

In fact, he is the first 'local' to head the court since the early 1900s. His immediate predecessor, the Earl of Malmesbury, had holdings at Hurn but that lies beyond the Forest's western boundary. With Berry Beeches to the west, Soarley Beeches to the east, South Oakley Inclosure in front and Backley Plain behind, the Old House must be the most cardiac of all Forest residences.

Certainly, Sir Dudley likes to feel – and quite rightly – that the Forest bloodstream circulates through and around his beautiful home.

'My door is always open,' he says. 'And I say that very conscious of how – corny – it sounds. But anybody with a problem or a grievance can bring it right to me – and that's better than waiting until the next time I come down from the other side of Winchester, or somewhere.

'If I hear that an animal grazing on the Forest is giving cause for concern, I can go and see for myself – though, of course, the normal procedure would be to dispatch an agister' – the Court has four full-time officials, each with his area to cover. 'I meet the people and I try to get to know their names. It is a matter of returning the courtesy because the chances are that they know my name.

'If you were to ask me what I consider to be my most valuable asset for the Forest, I would say my presence – and that should be a major consideration for any Official Verderer.

'It happens that I have had the privilege of meeting some very important people during my diplomatic career and I have developed friendships which have worked in a positive way for the good of the Forest on occasions.'

Such friendships were useful for protecting the status quo when, for instance, Hampshire County Council in 1973 were seeking to curtail (if not usurp) the Verderers' power with their New Forest Bill. That never got beyond the committee stage at Westminster.

In the late 1960s, before his appointment as Official Verderer, Sir Dudley was a prime mover in the opposition to a Forestry Commission programme which foresaw the removal of all hardwoods to make room for the more profitable softwoods – a furore which came to a head when the then Deputy

Surveyor, Dallas Mithen, ordered wholesale felling of beeches at Rushpole, one of the most picturesque of Ytene's woodlands. The actual success of the saviours in that episode could not be reckoned without mention of people like David Stagg and Jean Main Cobb, but it cannot be doubted that their voices were the louder for the amplification provided by Sir Dudley.

But he hasn't always been on the side of the conservationist.

'A few years ago, I was riding in Ridley Wood and there was a lot of dead wood lying around. It all looked a bit untidy. So, I had a quiet word with the Deputy Surveyor and said, "How about cleaning it up? When you get around to it – no hurry."

'Well, in a reasonable amount of time, he sent a couple of chaps up there and made the place look a bit more presentable – and the next thing I knew, here was this naturalist chap knocking on my door and asking me if I realised I had wiped out the only Forest habitat of the great spotted thingummy – that wasn't its name, but something like that. It just goes to show the truth of that line about not being able to please all the people all the time . . .'

But it was a lesson well learned. There are few Forest problems which look the same to all parties – and few decisions that will meet with universal acclaim.

Sir Dudley sips his sweet sherry and shifts toes in slippers. 'I don't know how to say this without sounding . . . immodest. But I've got perhaps five years to go in this position (damn me, I could drop dead tomorrow) and I worry about who will come next. I would like it to be someone – well – someone in a similar position to myself, someone on the spot.'

And what would he like to see done ahead of that sad succession?

'This is just a personal view because I know people in my court who would speak as strongly against it as I am for it. But I would like to see a merging of the Verderers and the New Forest Consultative Panel.'

Oof! I can hear the indrawn breaths from here. Sir Dudley was chairman of the Panel when he became Official Verderer and many were the protests that he could not reasonably fill both berths. The protestors at that time, jealous of any situation that might remove the initiative from the Court, foresaw an annexing of functions and were not happy.

At present, the Verderers are in session every six weeks or so and the Consultative Panel meet monthly around a table in the office of the Deputy Surveyor, Donn Small. Though the one is a unique vessel of public justice and the other is supposedly a consideration of Forest matters at expert level, there are faces and attitudes common to both bodies. What could be gained by blending the two?

'Though I get on very, very well with the Deputy Surveyor and nothing I say should be related to him personally, it is a fact that the Forestry Commission are not awfully good on letting people know what is happening. If such a merger would do anything to improve communications, that would be a gain.'

Things – and Foresters – being what they are, Sir Dudley's other ambition would also spark controversy. If people are touchy about the Forestry Commission, they are positively piebald about ponies.

In bloodline terms, there is just one class of New Forest pony, whether bred on the Forest or raised in stud – and yet the variation between animals can be immense. The argument goes back a long way, as I have outlined in a later chapter, and what Sir Dudley would like to see is a recognised distinction between those ponies who browse the furzy waste and those who never leave the green, green grass of home . . . some distinction, that is, which would favour the authentic status of the Commoner's beast and its peculiar strengths and send its more sophisticated offshoot off in search of a new classification.

And more . . . At the moment, when the Verderers find an animal on the Forest in a sorry condition, all they can do is to order its removal to the home of the Commoner owner – where it may or may not be given the means to

Ponies of the Forest. Sir Dudley Forwood, the Official Verderer, would like to put them in a class of their own.

recover. Sir Dudley wants to see that power extended to incorporate a back-up facility – so that if the Verderers discover the animal is actually in a worse condition for being taken off the Forest, they can order either remedial action or destruction in a humane fashion – and send the Royal Society for the Prevention of Cruelty to Animals along to administer any recourse in law where applicable. 'I would like us to be able to bring an end to suffering,' he says. 'Not just enable it to be removed from the public gaze.'

The Forwood love of creatures goes deep and is manifested in practical terms – although his affectionate nature draws a line at the fox.

When The Old House, vintage 1966, was taking shape and a bulldozer hired for the day was still within the reach of the ordinary man, Sir Dudley ordered a duckpond for the garden. It is kidney-shaped with an island in the middle and a stark, dead tree at the centre of the island. There the ducks – mallard, Muscovy and one dark lady of the sonnets who has managed to seduce most kinds of resident drake – have learned to roost in the night.

Time was when the peacocks had the same idea, utilising the then healthy tree. But the strain was too much for it. Whenever a peacock perches now, a little more of the skeleton breaks away – and these birds of paradise have taken to the house-tops.

The guinea-fowl, however, just don't learn; once there were eight and now there are three, while the local tods have developed a taste for occasional exotica.

You cannot tell Sir Dudley Forwood anything about the plundering fox – and you would be hard put to inform him, either, on the matter of daffodils. He plants a dozen bulbs a day – and has yellow spears streaking skyward in different parts of his garden from March through May.

At one Chelsea Flower Show, a spliced bloom took his fancy and he – loosely – ordered a couple of dozen.

'One hundred pounds,' said the grower.

'For two dozen?' inquired the surprised Sir Dudley.

'Each,' answered the grower. Sir Dudley promptly withdrew his order, considering £2,400 a rather high price for whimsy.

'Then he said to me' – Sir Dudley recalls the instance with a smile and a slight breathlessness as though he remains moved by it all – '"You really want that, don't you?" And he put a bulb in my hand. Sometimes, people surprise me with their – goodness.'

But he had no need to purchase the host which cover the soil near his southern fence as solid as custard. They have been there since Auberon Herbert planted them in 1906. 'There's many an old-timer has had a laugh with me over those,' says Sir Dudley. 'I don't know how many of them have told me, "I wouldn't have been here at all if my father hadn't brought my mother up to see Mr Herbert's daffodils".'

One glance at the thick and lasting woodlands beyond the fence gives the sense to that comment and the rustic revels that ensued when privacy was assured.

On our way back past the pond, Sir Dudley's eye is caught by a flash of white. 'Good grief . . . One of my ducks is dead!' No – it's a sliced bread wrapper. Probably a leftover from last Sunday when Sir Dudley and Lady Forwood opened their garden in aid of the St John Ambulance Society and raised a proud £67.

But litter at the Old House? Not even the Hon Auberon's gypsies did that.

Beginnings

WHEN we talk of 'ancient and ornamental woodlands' and point to seasoned trunks which may well carry Tudor, Plantagenet, Stuart, Hanoverian memories within their rings, we tend to think of them as providing the oldest part of the Forest. But the real antiquity lies beneath our feet.

For aeons, the only incident to be recorded was a rise in sea level, a dip in land, a shift of axis, and while there was nobody to write it down, the rocks made an accounting of their own.

In recent years, we have sought to pigeon-hole this indeterminate period with titles like Eocene, Oligocene, Pleistocene and that somehow renders it all so remote that we can hardly believe it was actually happening *here*.

What we forget or at least fail to appreciate is that the event we trace in this chalk downfold of the Hampshire Basin has only one word which makes sense of time and that word is Now. All the past is Now, when it is happening. . . .

Now, great rivers roll out of the Wiltshire downlands, straddling the basin (if it is not a line of downs in itself), licking, leaching, denuding, finding only the toughest rock immune.

Now, the earth shrugs its shoulders and the sea is creaming up to those same downs, bringing its rubbish with it, sand and clay.

Now, the fresh water has the advantage again but the old wide river beds are gone, altered by the sheer weight of the previous occupant. Instead, those springs must gather strength until their very persistence wears them estuarine paths through salt marshes to the sea.

Now, the outcrops are in the teeth of the glaciers which chew and grind and fill their maws with splinters. Now, a state of summer releases that grip and washes gravel down to new lodgings on the banks of an Avon as broad as the Amazon.

And with the ice sheet gradually retreating towards the north, so our story really begins. Because here, moving almost as fast as the melting line, come the TREES. Tundra type, first of all, to join the lichens which are already established in defiance of overwhelming odds – mosses and other low growers like bilberry and cowberry; stunted bushes of birch and willow.

A pause for breath in our headlong flight through prehistory. We are within ten thousand years of today – a mere blink to those whose answer to every evolutionary anomaly is to add another million years to the calendar. See how different things are already – and yet see, too, that nothing has changed but the people. Radio-carbon dating began it, infra-red photography continues it, progress confirms . . . that the world is not as old as it used to be.

The first straight trunks were no-stunt birches and pines and they spread right across Britain and Ireland because St George's Channel was still a rift of the future. It is likely that all drier ground, excepting mountain reaches, had evergreen cover mixed with birch and, in the meantime, willow found a footing on waterlogged low ground.

Hazel came next from the southern part of the Continent, mobilised by the warming climate. Oak, elm, lime and alder followed and by the time ash, beech and hornbeam had made their way here, the sylvan march was losing impetus.

It is at this point that the relationship between the overgrown flowers which we call trees and the soil varieties produced by the successive conditions I have summarised began to dictate selectivity. Oak, ash and hazel, by virtue of their adaptability, were able to spread wherever the forces of dispersal took them. Wych elm and alder covered the distance but not in the same density. Beech, lime, common elm and hornbeam would have stayed more or less where they landed in Southern England, but for their introduction elsewhere by man. Of the original all-encompassing pine forests, only a few segments now remain and they are in Scotland.

Nobody at this time was taking notes. So how do we know?

The short answer is – peat.

Peat is a wonderful, versatile substance and one which has never been in short supply in the New Forest. It comprises an amalgam of partly decomposed plant remains – mostly water plants, like reeds, sedges or bog moss. When they die, these plants cannot rot away completely because the cold swamps where they grow are very short on oxygen, which is essential to decay. In these stagnant, airless conditions, layer packs down upon layer of plant remains and, over the centuries, the depth of peat can reach twenty to thirty feet.

Peat also has preserving qualities which would have made the Egyptian undertakers green. There are few bogside communities in the Forest – or, indeed, anywhere else – which do not have their story of the horse, cart, driver and all who disappeared into the soggy blackness, only to be dredged up somehow a generation later with flesh intact. The marshy bottom which follows the road between Holmsley and Wilverly, for instance, is said to have swallowed up a full-size Army tank.

The hazards are clear. But how can peat be helpful?

If trees could love, their affairs would have to be conducted by letter. The order for all living things to reproduce according to their kind was never so random as in this case. They relied upon bees and breezes to bear the microscopic pollen grains each primeval spring from male flower to female. It was – and remains – the most star-crossed and haphazard of arrangements and works only because, in the vast number of grains released, some few must eventually find their way to the proper destination.

Those that fall by the wayside are not reproducers, but reporters. In our day, here comes a botanist with a metal tube several metres long. He plunges it into a peat bog, boring on until the bottom is reached. When the rod is withdrawn, it has taken a cross-section of the plant remains from current spring to remote past. Back in his laboratory, with leisure and a microscope, he can set to work on an interpretation of his material, aided by the fact that the pollen of each tree is distinctive by size and shape.

Near the bottom of his probe, he will find pine, willow and birch. Higher up, hazel, oak, elm, ash and alder are evident. Near the top – if the setting is ancient and ornamental – pine and birch have given way to beech and pedunculate oak.

In valley bottoms near the more recent Forest inclosures, the sequence may differ slightly in the higher stages, with the pinus sylvestris overlaid by such exotics as Japanese larch and western hemlock, Sitka spruce and California redwood. But these latter elaborations are entirely due to the machinations of man – and perhaps we should go back a little way now to see just when it was he entered the equation.

Felling pines. Pollen samples show conifers are the most ancient as well as the most recent of Forest Trees.

First civilisations (Old Stone Age) would have been likely to avoid the Forest for the most part, because their simple implements were not equal to the task of clearing it or making even any noticeable impact upon it. They were hunters and pursuit brought peril in itself because the bogs were waiting and were not at all choosy in their victims. Meat was a feast and the more likely repast was edible roots – what a trial and error that must have been – brambles, crab apples, nuts in season.

As the climate improved, so the Mesolithic (Middle Stone Age) man began to make his presence felt upon the Forest's heathland areas. He still had no craft beyond an increasing skill in survival and his produce came more from toil than from soil. There was no sanctity in death for him – a dead man lay where he fell or suffered the most superficial of coverings until Nature could undertake the rest – with the result that, from a population point of view, Mesolithic man was probably far more prevalent than any visible evidence would indicate.

It was not until the influx of a distinct physical type, dark and short in stature, from Mediterranean Europe, that a degree of sophistication began to show – and the most precocious action Neolithic man took was to turn the soil. From then on, he went from refinement to refinement – crops, animal husbandry, art forms, a more killing type of weapon.

For some reason, New Stone Age sites in the Forest are less in evidence than those of their predecessors, though occasional axehead finds would seem to indicate that they did at least send hunting parties into the Hampshire veldt.

By this time, Hengistbury Head, westward border of the Stour/Avon estuary, was gaining importance as a port. But from there, tracks inland to centres of population on the Wessex chalk seem to have skirted the Forest.

One can speculate on the reasons for this. It is feasible that man's journey towards civilisation was paralleled by his progress into mayhem. The Forest was (and still is) a good place for an ambush and there were surely those who already believed that there were easier ways than working to make a living. The paths up into the downlands show a distinct tendency to avoid valley bottoms and it is certain the hardy Neolith was more concerned with seeing what lay ahead (and behind) than getting his feet wet.

New knowledge flowed from the European mainland as fast as the tide and a fair wind could carry it, and Bronze Age man was entirely able to cope with the conditions which greeted him on the lowland where he beached his craft.

The Archaeology Division of the Ordnance Survey Office have listed more than 170 round barrows dating from that era – 2,000 B.C. downwards – in the Forest and it is a shame that the most extensive record should be in burial grounds. It is like a book which contains only full-stops. Heywood Sumner, in loving and painstaking work in the 1920 and 1930s, led the way to most of these – and described them, in fact, with an excitement that rather gives the lie to my 'full-stop' statement. But no matter.

Far more optimistic, to my mind, have been the field studies since by Anthony Pasmore, E.L. Jones and Colin Tubbs, who were looking not for signs of death but for signs of life. The phrase 'fieldwork' would be right in this sense if it were never used in any other. They followed their noses, their instincts and certain regularities of the terrain to unveil enclosures and systems of cultivation.

One green bank looks much like another and there is no surefire way of distinguishing a mediaeval enclosure from one of a far earlier date, except perhaps in its proximity to one or more of the barrows mentioned. But the point is not vital because the primitive plantings were already setting a pattern that would be followed right up to the 19th century of the Christian Era.

After Bronze came Iron and, again, a drop in discernible population. Colin Tubbs has suggested *(The New Forest: An Ecological History, David & Charles, 1968)* that the fluctuations are related directly to the state of the soil and that the Bronze Age or even earlier innovation of felling and clearing by fire may well have left the land less fertile for the Iron Age newcomers.

On the other hand, the forts which are primary evidence of Iron Age activity in the Forest – Castle Hill, Burley; Roe Wood, Malwood Castle, Tachbury Mount, Godmanescap, Godshill Wood, Buckland Rings, Ampress, Exbury and Matley Heath – may well also reflect a communal desire to consolidate on the better ground.

Romano-British traces reveal an extensive pottery industry related geographically to clay deposits in the north of the Forest – Latchmore Brook, Dockens Water, Ashley Hole – and near Burley. But although a Roman village existed at Nursling, east of the Forest, and a 156 lb pig of lead, inscribed as the property of the Emperor Nero, was unearthed at Bossington, no real inroads were made by the Latin conquerors. They camped as militia at Buckland Rings and adapted and administered local potteries – but they built their villas elsewhere.

The next settlers with any idea of permanence were the Jutes (one rendering of 'Ytene' is 'Land of the Jutes'), utilising existing settlements and concentrating on war and agriculture. Not guns and butter but possibly swords and milk.

Then came the West Saxons, landing in 495 A.D. at 'Cerdices ora', variously identified as Hamble, Calshot, Totton, but certainly at some handy point where the Southampton Water narrows to become the River Test. They took on the British at 'Natanleay' (Anglo-Saxon Chronicle), probably Netley Marsh, and then pushed on to 'Cerdices ford', now Charford, just south of Downton. From this insurgence grew the kingdom of Wessex, with its capital at Winchester and its destiny to lead all England.

These were the Celts, dark, swarthy, secretive, and the true Forester, says Brian Vesey-Fitzgerald, is just like them. 'They are solid as the Romany is solid, but as the Romany is not, they are also stolid and silent. . . . That is the form of their independence. It comes, I think, from living in dark and silent places and knowing the spirits that live among tall trees.'

When I was wondering what authenticity I might claim for pretending any kind of familiarity with the Forest nuances, that observation was heartening. For I am a Celt, dark where the hair remains, swarthy enough to have a five o'clock shadow by four p.m., silent when I should be otherwise, as solid as sixteen stone . . . but over six feet tall, just to make a nonsense of the genetics. And if I do not 'know the spirits that live among tall trees', certainly I feel them. That will be my answer to all blond-haired 'natives' who call me popinjay.

At this point, we move from pre-history into history and perhaps it is time to introduce another 'popinjay' – who, in ten years, has probably done more to uncover the Forest personality than a dozen locals in a dozen lifetimes.

Underneath the Archives

DAVID J. STAGG, middle-grade civil servant who prefers his Department to remain anonymous, and Sir Dudley Forwood, Official Verderer and friend of Royalty, are great pals. The circumstance is an eloquent confirmation of the strange harmony of contrasts which is the strength of the grass-roots interests in the Forest.

Sir Dudley lives in a stately home but David lives in a homely state. When I met him in his small 1930s villa off the Ashurst to Bartley road, there was just enough light left to view a garden where bluebells, if not exactly rioting, were certainly in civil disorder.

David, in his early forties, lives the bachelor life with his dog and his books. And such books . . .

If I had not torn myself from the titles with a conscious physical effort, I should be there yet. Four, five, six editions of John R. Wise's *The New Forest: Its History and Scenery*, each one grander than the last; the children's books that Heywood Sumner illustrated between his hammer-taps upon New Forest barrows and potteries; William Gilpin's *Remarks on Forest Scenery*; Hutchinson and Crespigny, Cornish, Moore, Begbie, Willingham Rawnsley, bound in leather, tooled in gold. Gerald Lascelles's *Thirty Five Years in the New Forest* – 'that's changing hands for £18 now,' I told him and he smiled as though £1,800 would not tempt the work from him.

There cannot be any finer collection of Forest memorabilia but still he keeps expanding it. I had fifty-ish Forest books and thought I could name about twenty-five more. One rapid and lecherous look at the shelves and I kept my mouth shut – except to address the generous whisky which he provided.

For all that, David Stagg's obsession is not with the published but with the unpublished.

He moved into the Forest just over a decade ago and plunged straight into controversy. The Rushpole Wood episode was just gathering impetus – it is explained in more detail towards the end of the next chapter – and David took his stand on the side of the angels with a contribution that would have been industrial espionage at Queen's House, Lyndhurst, but was merely opportunism at Alice Holt Forest.

The first attraction had been of a conservationist nature. Now, with the dust settling on that altercation, David sought to give his interest a pedigree.

Hodge And His Masters, the Richard Jefferies essays on the social revolution in the countryside, first interested David in the lot of the agricultural labourer, and when he tried to satisfy that curiosity in a local way by frequent visits to the Hampshire Records Office in Winchester he soon discovered that there were no records readily available. Such documents as existed were penned by a variety of hands which had apparently successfully shaken off the finesse of the monastery and in a pidgin Latin that would have been barely understood in Rome.

In school, years earlier, David had taken Latin for a handful of terms. Now, he set about turning that slight start into the key to a mystery.

He concentrated on the century from 1240 to 1340, approximately, because that was the first period which provided a sufficient number of documents to indicate any kind of consistency.

He found that the immensity of the task made the Dead Sea Scrolls look like Janet and John. He found that the Latin passages themselves were simple enough, even allowing for the mediaeval manner. Where he ran into trouble was with the idiosyncrasies of the scribes, the tricks of phrase, the 'twiddly bits', as he calls them. And where the project ran out of joy was when, in translation, he discovered very little drama; merely a system of penalty and litigation that was even more long-winded than the procedures we criticise today.

But for half-a-dozen years David has kept it interesting for himself. And only now, as – at the time of my visit – he struggles with the intricacies of a card-index system to provide a quick and easy guide to all his slow, hard labour, is Stagg beginning to flag.

'It became a kind of treasure hunt with names and places,' he said, wilfully clearing a space on a paper-laden table to make room for glass and elbows.

'I found that spellings tended to change between one sheet and the next, and not only because the scribes themselves changed. The different versions mattered little to them in their own time because they all knew what they were talking about and most of the actual exchanges between parties were verbal and colloquial, with very little regard for the man in the corner who was trying to take notes.

'The records were just to chronicle precedents and a lot of the time they were only aids to memory. I don't suppose anybody then pictured me now hunched over a hot Latin primer and a cold Teacher's trying to piece together the history of the movement.'

Many of the matters are incomplete and there is nothing distinctly and distinctively 13th century about the issues that emerge. Complaints of Common rights violated, land wrenched from peasants and tickled from lords, taxes unpaid, quotas not met lie alongside details of reparations made, fines paid and charges laid.

The Hampshire Records Office plan publication of David's findings and the true value can be summarised thus – a sizeable gap has been filled in the availability of public knowledge; because of a man and a mission and more than a little midnight oil, there now exist full details of a much earlier Hodge and his Masters.

And David Stagg? No fear of him being at a loose end.

Having given his acquired scholarship to the 13th and 14th centuries, he now moves on to the 17th and 18th.

Already, he is surrounding himself with volumes on the art and science of penmanship, sorting his 'fs' from his 'ss', reading up on the history of the hand-written word . . . because mediaeval Latin is like copperplate to decipher compared with the rigours of Hanoverian English.

He showed me examples, I gave him my condolences and we had another whisky . . .

Wheat from Chaff

IN a nonacentenary celebration of the inclosure, it would be comforting to have heavier confirmation of the date – a year, let alone a day. That is lacking.

John R. Wise – *The New Forest: Its History and Scenery* – sets the date of the action at 1079 but gives no positive source for the statement (though he pinpoints just about everything else in footnotes which threaten to push the running text off the page).

A Charter is supposed to have existed in the time of Canute, but it has been suggested that this was an early Norman forgery to honour piracy with precedent. Indeed, the suggestion is as likely to be a fabrication as the fraud it purports to expose. As we shall see elsewhere, neither rich man nor poor man, neither Church nor State could be relied upon for truth where it conflicted with self-interest.

This much at least is definite – by 1086, the date of the Domesday compilation, this was unquestionably a Royal Forest, and the fact is underlined by a special section in the Hampshire folios entitled 'In Nova Foresta et Circa Ea' – 'In The New Forest And Around It'.

The first historians had no time for statistical evidence when they were setting up their accounts to conform with post-William and anti-William thinking; and in that, they were supported through many centuries by narrators more swayed by defamation than by detail.

Thus, Florence of Worcester speaks in general terms of men driven from their homes, fields laid waste, houses and churches destroyed; Orderic Vitalis declares the district to have been thickly inhabited and states that William ruined no less than 60 parishes; Walter Mapes puts the toll at 36 mother churches destroyed – but then says that William Rufus, *son* of the Conqueror, created the Forest.

More recently, Lappenberg (*England Under the Anglo-Norman Kings*) describes the Forest as 'the most thriving part of England' and insists that William 'mercilessly caused churches and villages to be burnt down within its circuit'. He also cites the Conqueror's 'bloody sacrifice' and 'glaring cruelty towards the numerous inhabitants'.

Is this, then, what we celebrate?

Hardly. Florence, Vitalis, Mapes and any others who trod their footsteps could have done a proper job by taking themselves to the Treasury at Winchester (or later, London) and making a proper inquiry.

William Cobbett's destruction of these claims at a literal level is almost as well-known as the allegations themselves and is available in so many other places (including his *Rural Rides*) that there would be little value in quoting it here. But his zeal as a disputist does, in fact, misdirect him into the occasional sweeping statement himself. I hardly think his seven-mile ride from Lyndhurst to Beaulieu, largely across Matley Heath and Denny Lodge, justifies his observation – 'so that a poorer spot than the New Forest there is not in all England, nor, I believe, in the whole world'. What I believe is that he could not have turned his eyes westward for the whole of that seven miles, and perhaps he didn't open them at all.

In any event, cutting through the undergrowth of Saxon, Whig and Liberal persuasion, we find the suggestion that the couple of pages left for the Nova Foresta entries proved nothing like enough to list the many holdings which existed within and on the outskirts of the Forest, so that the scriveners (recounts Lord Kenchington in *The Commoners' New Forest*) had to find space on other scrolls, using different ink to make a very necessary qualification.

Domesday names 108 places – manors, villages, hamlets – in the Forest, of which about 30 were entirely absorbed into the royal precinct. Of most of the rest, only the outer edges were taken, probably in some mediaeval 'green belt' strategy.

In fact, the figures involved in the Conqueror's 'laying waste' seem to add up to about 17,000 acres removed from settlement or growth. In valuation terms, this reduced the size of the district from $212\frac{1}{2}$ hides to 72 and its rateable value from about £338 to about £133. So William's encompassing move lost him revenue at a time when the £1 in your pocket was worth infinitely more than it is today.

As for his 'glaring cruelty towards the numerous inhabitants', we find, for instance, that Ulviet, formerly a royal huntsman to King Harold and a considerable land-holder, lost a little of his estates but still retained the trust of the new monarch. A royal huntsman he remained. And Aelfric, another large holder of the Saxon line, continued as tenant of lands his uncle and father had held before him at Brockenhurst. Furthermore, in compensation for such of his land that passed into William's hands, he was given another estate at Milford.

Waleran, a huntsman, Osbern, a falconer, Agemund at Wellow, Alwi at Midgham, Picot at Burgate, Gozelin at Breamore and quite a list of Saxon thanes suffered nibbling to their boundaries but certainly not the edge of a Norman sword.

William's Forest laws were simple but effective; for killing a deer, death; for shooting at a deer and missing, loss of hands; for disturbing a deer, loss of sight.

The penalties seem extreme. But consider this – even allowing for the fact that William had none of the conservationist's care for the species (and perhaps he did: the Chronicler says he 'loved the tall stags as if he were their father'), he still had more interest in them than had those who sought to offend his laws. Poachers were after one thing – meat. The royal hunter was after two – a quarry at the right time and the perpetuity of his pleasure, so that as well as the sport there had to be concern for welfare. And perhaps he didn't trust a man with a bow in the Forest. Certainly, the subsequent experience of his family in that area indicated the need for the strongest caution that could be applied.

The penalties in themselves were not peculiar to Forest infringements – they had been in existence since the invention of a blade sharp enough to do the job. And there were to be worse violations for lesser crimes as history took its course.

No, the real resentment was at the demarcation. Outside Forest boundaries, a commoner could bring down a deer without retribution. Thus, poachers tried to drive the deer across the boundaries – and then cried the odds when failure cost them hands or eyes.

William II did nothing to alter the legal situation, but showed such a predilection for hunting in the New Forest that it was possible to plan and execute his assassination there without too much concern for the unpredictable. In fact, the plot was so well-circulated before the event that churchmen were able to give a special piquance to their 'wrath of God' sermons. We shall study the killing in more detail later. Sufficient to say that, as an upshot of it, Henry I avoided the Forest like the plague throughout his reign – though he was the first monarch to concede 'right of warren' to certain subjects whose estates lay within Forest boundaries. Under this right, they might hunt and kill fox, wolf, wildcat, hare, badger and squirrel.

It has been suggested, and often, that this concession had the object of removing those predators which provided a threat to deer and wild boar. But there is more to it than that. Hare, rabbit, badger and squirrel did not jeopardise the beasts of the chase in any way. What they did do was to menace crops which were already undergoing severe limitations. Henry's decision was more likely made on those grounds, and under pressure, than from any desire to satisfy the hunting instincts of the villein classes.

Henry II extended the boundaries of the royal forests, putting even more pressure on cultivation.

Richard I, who had needs of his own, and most of them financial, found a way of killing two birds with one stone. He would authorise disafforestation at a price – and that price would keep him in coin for his ventures abroad. At the same time, purely for his public relations image, one suspects, he abolished the dire penalties for actual and attempted poaching. The serfs would be so grateful, he reasoned, that they would be glad to follow him to the Crusades – and let the Saracens take their hands, their eyes and their lives.

John thought the idea of profit from disafforestation so good that he made it his own, though ensuring that none of his own particular pleasure grounds – the New Forest included – should be hived off in this way.

The boy king, Henry III, made his Charta de Foresta more or less at the dictation of the barons, still feeling their muscles after Runnymede. The document has been said to have brought a new humanity to the running of royal forests, but that would be pitching sophistication a little high for the eleven-year-old Henry. What actually happened was that the barons took (or took back) the bits they wanted and allowed the Crown to keep the rest – including the New Forest.

Ten years later, in 1227, Henry was in a much stronger position and the reafforestation process began rolling again. But Henry, no great lover of hunting, began to show more concern for the vert (the greenery) than the venison. Eclipse of the royal deer still carried usual imprisonment, but the offences now considered major were chopping and lopping – a nice juxtaposition from woodlander to woodland.

Edward I extended forest boundaries, too, much to the chagrin of families who had, perhaps, seen their holdings passing into and out of their hands with something approaching regularity. Complaints against the king's new perambulations became the most common cause of dissent, and in 1277 Edward ordered a fresh perambulation, which returned to the forest-dwellers much of the land which their forefathers – the 'honest and lawful men' of the Charta de Foresta – had won. This time, the New Forest was not affected, or again 20 years later. But in 1300 the expanse was reduced considerably, for no apparent reason. The land freed had no cultivation value and little work was done on it.

What happened now was that a periphery had been created which interested neither Crown nor Commoner. Certainly, it laid dormant the question of shifting boundaries for the next five centuries and more – and when the Crown came back in an encompassing mood, it was as an agency of administration and not an expression of majestic whim. During that interval, successive monarchs began to concern themselves with what went on within the perambulation defined by the Parliament at Lincoln in 1300.

The poor soil of the New Forest was not entirely its salvation but was definitely responsible for various stays of execution.

For instance, by 1483, such inroads had been made into other forests for building timber that it was necessary to prepare Parliament's first piece of legislation designed to protect and replace pressurised woodland. The experts had discovered that once a tree was gone, it would not grow again while wildlife could devour seedlings.

How true this was of the New Forest is a matter for conjecture. As stated, its riches were not in its soil, so that settlement here would have been much slower than in the areas of the Midland Forest of Arden and the Kent and Sussex Weald . . . and possibly of a more clandestine nature.

I mentioned earlier primitive plantings that were setting a pattern to be followed right into the 19th century. One word for these might be 'encroachments'. The sinister principle was adopted by the high (or fairly high) as well as the lowly, and it occurred in two ways, depending whether you had a fence of your own to move or whether you had any land at all.

With the landed resident, it was a languid and little-by-little exercise of the 'rolling powers' that he was to decry later in government. If a fence needed replacing – well, move it outward a few feet. Absorb that neighbouring clearing which was only a temptation to the deer, after all, to come into your patch and plough up your victuals. And if the king was otherwise engaged with affairs of state or a war, it might be years before anyone in authority brought a measuring rod to your land.

With the no-account, the deal was different, far more bare-faced cheek than a calculated risk. But there was a tradition that if he could raise a hearth and a roof overnight and surround it with a bank, the squatter might stay.

And if he could maintain this precarious foothold for 21 years – then it was his.

The 1483 Act, which allowed inclosure of denuded areas for seven-year periods, almost gave the blessing to the arrangement. In the first few subsequent years, 5,800 acres of the New Forest were utilised in this way – ditches dug, banks raised and topped with bramble and roots put down – tree and person, so to speak.

Suddenly, everybody was recognising the value of timber. Queen Elizabeth I wanted it kept in good fettle for shipbuilding. James I started off with maritime use in mind but too soon found standing timber a convenient and plentiful substitute for cash to settle his debts. Charles I picked up the 'windfall' habit. Cromwell, by contrast, just let the trees rot. Charles II found in the broadleaves good currency for his indulgences. James II barely had time to view the ruins of the Stuart estates before events of a far more pressing nature overtook him.

William III produced a stabilising force with his Act of 1698, which provided for the immediate planting of 2,000 acres in the New Forest and a further 200 acres a year, with a final figure of 6,000 acres. His priority need was for timber to replace a decaying fleet, and though he surely knew that the consequences of his verdant investment would not be clear in his lifetime, he realised that these trees he was taking out now would have to be put back if the Forest was to have a future at all. (Unfortunately, the hurricane of 1703 was going to bring a major setback. Woodward puts the toll at 4,000 of the 'best oaks' laid low by the storm.)

Commoners' reaction to what amounted to a licence to close off whatever of 'their' land (it was Crown land) might be required dropped the boom on William's good intentions. In the first 15 years after the Act, only 1,022 acres were planted and it was 1750 before another 250 acres were added. But some form of words must have been found during the next quarter century because in 1776, a further 2,066 acres were planted.

If the Commoners had known then what they know now, it is unlikely that any promise would have swayed them from total opposition.

It was in 1776, as an experiment, that Scots pine was introduced to the Forest in two small plots at Bolderwood and Ocknell. And in the intervening 200-odd years, the Scots pine has proved itself the Forester's dream, near enough, and the Commoner's nightmare. It grows quickly, spreads (the Commoner would say) like wildfire and has certainly generated more flare-ups between Crown and tenant than any other single item. Each year, the Forestry Commission destroys what it considers a reasonable number of trees. Each year, the Commoner complains that the quota is not enough. The Commoners view its unchecked spread across heath and moorland as a

The Knightwood Oak – its shape was determined by the 17th century practice of 'pollarding' or lopping main branches to spread growth.

Commission conspiracy; the Commission point out that they cannot control the birds or the breeze.

And a lot of the time, the Scots pine itself is the villain, for it chooses to grow in areas largely unreachable by pedestrian means, defies the fire-raisers, official and otherwise, and delivers its seeds to avian and airstream. But . . . two centuries ago, its value was as a rapid developer with a protective nature and by 1848 it was in regular use as a shelter belt alongside broadleaf nurseries.

The deer had always been a blight on the efforts of both sides, and in 1851 Queen Victoria enunciated the Deer Removal Act, apparently as an answer to the growing lobby of complainants among the Commoners. As it turned out, the 'deer removal' bit was the carrot – and the stick was a proviso which allowed the Crown to inclose a further 10,000 acres for timber production.

As these trees matured and the plantations were thrown open, so another 10,000 acres might be inclosed. It was not clear from the legislation whether that was to be manifested once or ad infinitum and the Crown was not in a hurry to clarify the ambiguity. Living an existence that was seldom better than hand to mouth, few of the Commoners were able to put the law to the test at a level which would have been necessary to bring about any change. The situation was not eased by the attitude of the then Deputy Surveyor, young Lawrence Henry Cumberbatch, who possessed that mercurial quality that would come to be called 'dynamic' and whose first consideration was to get those 10,000 acres under seed – which he did between 1851 and 1868 – regardless of any other factor.

But now the Commoners were discovering strange bedfellows – gentry whose own holdings within the Forest were being jeopardised by the energy of Mr Cumberbatch – people who had 'clout'.

In 1871, the House of Commons declared that no more old trees were to be felled and no new inclosures made pending an inquiry into the whole situation. A Select Committee was set up in 1875 and from its recommendations grew the New Forest Act, 1877. This set a limit of 16,000 acres on Crown inclosures, gave status to the Commoners in the exercise of their rights and reconstituted the ancient Court of Verderers to articulate the Commoners' case in all deliberations.

Three years later, Cumberbatch retired and there are those who suggest, even today, that the Act struck a personal blow to his single-mindedness. In 31 years, he had become a symbol of opposition to Commoner intentions and there were few regrets when he went on his way.

Anthony Pasmore, in his *Verderers of the New Forest* (Pioneer Publications Limited, 1977) states that the Select Committee's inquiries of

1875 had a damaging effect on Cumberbatch's mental state and that he returned from his session before them and ordered the destruction of any deer remaining in the Forest. Elsewhere, Pasmore talks about 'this vanquished and deranged champion of the Crown', although it must be said that the photograph he includes of Cumberbatch at a picnic on Bolderwood Green in 1883 shows a man at ease in the bosom of his family.

Whether Cumberbatch was a career forester who died a little inside when his best intentions were vaunted, or whether he was a misunderstood man whose ambitions were read as obsessions by those with whom they did not accord, remains unresolved. But this much must be admitted: he virtually made the Forest as we see it today. He planted a great deal of Scots pine which, for all its nuisance value, has had its uses in times of strife. The fine green Douglas firs which reach closest to the sky in the Rhinefield Ornamental Walks today began their journey upward in his time. More of his experiments with the unusual trees can be seen in Bolderwood. And a lot of the oak woodland on show also owes its beginnings to his efforts.

The history of the Forest since has been largely the history of its Deputy Surveyors.

The Hon Gerald Lascelles followed Cumberbatch into the hot seat and must have found himself very close to blisters as he set out to make the new Act work. Though the major points were clear, the minor ones were not – and the Commoners were gleeful indeed to trade on every knothole. Lascelles wanted Forest roads improved. The Commoners did not see the need, particularly since the most obvious benefit from the improvements would be to timber haulage . . . and to the new gentry, whom they didn't want, either.

Lascelles, being an aristocrat, had a natural sympathy with the landlords. At the same time, he had a comprehensive and not unfriendly appreciation of the smallholders' shallow purses.

The New Forest Highways Act, which he helped to fashion, gave the Crown the responsibility for putting the roads to rights, and thereafter they were to be maintained by the Road Boards. The Commoners were delighted. Then the roads became the responsibility of the Hampshire County Council – and the Commoners had to contribute to their upkeep via the rates. But it was better than handing over their hard-earned cash to the Office of Woods.

The fact that Lascelles should have finished his 35 years, regarded with such universal affection, is a tribute to the stature of the man himself because, as far as the records show, he was as often in confrontation with the Commoners as he was in harmony with them.

And there is evidence recently come to light that he was amused more

The Naked Man. This was a living tree according to Taylor's map of 1759, but it is dead and nearly gone today at Wilverley. Said to be the gibbet of one Mark Way, a highwayman, it is more likely a pun on 'marked way', the old Southampton-Dorset road.

than bemused by his own tenuous standing in such an ambivalent community. Among papers recently donated to the Verderers (and I thank Anthony Pasmore for drawing this to my attention) is this Savoyard scrap of doggerel in his handwriting.

Song of the Deputy Surveyor

If I gave permits free to the gay licensee,
And allowed him to shoot the grey hen,
And said, 'Without fear, you may kill all the deer',
Oh, should I be popular then?
If I sent them some foxes, securely in boxes,
And to Lyndhurst the carriage should pay,
If I cut no more planks on the green Holmsley banks,
Would that make me popular – eh?

And supposing that I should consume humble pie
And take back all I wrote with my pen,
And become an upholder of 'Moens of Boldre',
Oh, should I be popular then?
For I want to be popular, popular, popular!
And worshipped by all Forest men.
If I lie down and grovel in front of old Lovell,
Oh, should I be popular then?

The 'Moens' of the piece was W.C.J. Moens, an able and fluent spokesman for the Commoners at the turn of the century and 'old Lovell' was Francis Lovell of Hinchelsea, a founder member of the New Forest Association, cultural wing of the Commoners' defence organisation.

The verse fills one with a rather warm feeling about the Hon Gerald, and that was precisely how the Foresters felt about him when he retired in late 1914.

If Lascelles's concern had been for roads, that of his successor, Vernon Francis Leese (1914–25) was for drains – an enthusiasm which, with his promise early on of controlling the spread of seedling firs, could well have endeared him to the Commoners.

Unfortunately, there occurred a major diversion, in the form of World War 1. The old recognisable seesaw battle between those who sought to inclose and those determined to keep open became subordinate to the demands of the national emergency. The Forest, in common with the rest of the nation, was anxious to do all it could to kick the Kaiser – or at least, to offer the armed forces all accommodation at its disposal to that end.

The open woodland was soon pocked with camp-sites as the area became a staging zone for departures to the Continent. Manoeuvres followed – and the slit trenches and litter which resulted were accepted with the stiff upper lip characteristic of the period. The Verderers were generous with their permissions to the military authorities and some of the agreements were positively informal, a willingness which would emerge as a weakness when, at the cessation of hostilities, the locals got round to pressing the War Office for reinstatement of affected areas.

A grenade school at Bolton's Bench and an airfield at Beaulieu and their extensions were going to prove particularly troublesome to remove. But when an artillery range was mapped out between Matley and Decoy Pond without any reference to the Verderers at all, it became clear that the military were abusing their privileges, if not actually mauling the feeding hand.

Other irritations were beginning to show themselves. Animals were being lost because of gates left open, not to mention those which became casualties of the new regime which now spiked their habitual grazing grounds.

In August 1918, the Matley Trench Mortar School was replaced by a war dog training school, with the idea of training the animals to carry messages under battle conditions. Part of the instruction involved taking the dogs to various parts of the Forest and releasing them with messages to return to Matley. Within a few months, several Commoners' animals – pigs, in particular – had been killed and injured, and with the emergency now over, the Verderers wrote to the War Office demanding that the school should be closed and the losers compensated. The school closed in May 1919, but claims were not settled until November of that year.

Mr Leese's term of office yielded little else of controversy, except for the switch of power from the Office of Woods to the Forestry Commission under the Forestry (Transfer of Woods) Act, 1923.

The New Forest Advisory Committee was founded during the tenure of Lionel Sherbrooke Osmaston (1925–31) and extensive re-inclosure went ahead with protests from the Commoners but none from the Verderers, who were, it seemed, favourably impressed by the new peak in consultation which had been indicated by the committee.

In 1931 came David Young – in the 'strong-arm' mould of Gerald Lascelles, says Anthony Pasmore. Little is recorded of his activities between 1931 and 1939, but recollections are that he very soon made himself an invaluable adviser to the Verderers.

From 1939–45, the Forest was again in the grip of the military. Applications for land came and were granted and the consequences were much the same as they had been 25 years earlier, only more so. Three airfields, two bombing ranges, service installations, damaged bridges, slit trenches, barbed wire all over the Forest and a fair number of abandoned high explosives were the manifestations of military encroachments totalling 8,700 acres.

The War Office were not as fast to remove their trappings as they had been to fit them – and Young himself, on several occasions, expressed annoyance at the delay.

The length of his stay – 18 years – is as good an evidence as any of his ability to do the job to the satisfaction of the many factions he had to seek to appease. Allied against the desire to please, however, is the determination not to be pleased; facing a Deputy Surveyor's attempts to do something worth while is the Commoner's race memory that anything coming from the Crown must have a catch in it.

Through the Baker Committee – chaired by the Rt Hon Harold Trevor Baker – David Young, as secretary and more importantly man on the spot, was largely responsible for the report that led to the 1949 New Forest Act. Under Section 13, the Forestry Commission could now inclose Ancient and Ornamental Woodland, 20 acres at a time, with the approval of the Verderers, and reafforest it.

Says Anthony Pasmore: 'Young regarded Section 13 as the most important change to be brought about by the Act and, when questioned by Sir Roy Robinson (then chairman of the Forestry Commission) as to the wisdom of including the A&OW . . . declared the Act "gave us an opportunity at long last of putting these Woods into production". This was no doubt (there is, in fact, considerable doubt – P.T.) the unspoken motive behind the pressure for powers to "save the old woods" . . .'

Young himself, in an article contributed to the New Forest Forestry Commission Guide (published by the Stationery Office in 1951 and given a fourth edition in 1969) said: 'The area of what has been described as "Ancient and Ornamental Woods" was assessed in 1963 at 7,487 acres. Under the 1877 Act, the Forestry Commissioners had no power to do anything in these woods. This was rather tragic because nearly every winter a heavy snowstorm or gale brings a number of ancient monarchs crashing to the ground. Cattle and ponies, on the other hand, keep any natural regeneration closely grazed back. This means that the area of completely stocked woods has dwindled year by year. To allow these woods to disappear would constitute an irreparable loss . . .'

On the face of it, that would seem to be a perfectly reasonable supposition – the more of the broadleaves which fall, the fewer will be left.

The point not stressed when the Act is being harangued is that such small-scale inclosures needed Verderer approval – and the same Act which allowed this provision also changed the Verderer set-up so that half of the Verderers – five – are now elected Commoners. Furthermore, in any split decision on allowing Forestry Commission or Ministry of Agriculture to inclose Open Forest land, the F.C. or Min. of Ag. representative in the appointed half of the Verderers is not allowed to vote.

This failsafe has given the Commoners sufficient power to rule out any of the carpet-bagging of which they accuse the Commission . . . if they can agree among themselves to do that.

Eric Wynne-Jones succeeded David Young and stayed 10 years, much of the time struggling with other Government departments for the return of land taken for airfields, particularly Beaulieu, where grazing animals were being trapped by slamming doors in abandoned buildings and consequently starving to death. It wasn't until March 1960 that the Beaulieu installation was handed back to the Verderers – even then only narrowly missing an application to requisition it until time immemorial as a radar station.

From 1959 to 1968, the post of Deputy Surveyor was held by William Arthur Cadman, who managed to find more contentment within the leafy confines of the New Forest than any and all of his predecessors – and to be held in esteem himself by every one of the Forest factions. The lyrical reminiscences of his Forest years are recounted in his book, *Dawn, Dusk and Deer* (Country Life, 1966) and as a timber merchant he made a fine naturalist. Cadman's Pool, near Stoney Cross, takes its name because of a little water-plant he introduced in an effort to enhance oxygenation on Forest ponds. It is the only place where the plant survived, recalls present Deputy Surveyor Donn Small.

During his term of office, Cadman was an honorary member of the Commoners' Defence Association and the New Forest section of the Hampshire Field Society. On his departure, he received a joint presentation from Commoners' Defence, Pony Breeders and New Forest Associations – a momentous accord, in itself.

His going was attended with even further drama. The Forestry Commission had been considering structural changes, combining the office of New Forest Deputy Surveyor with that of South-East Conservator, and housing the whole framework in Queen's House, Lyndhurst. The infighting involved in this manoeuvre will never be known, but the result was that Arthur Cadman stood up at the November 1968 meeting of the Verderers' Court and announced calmly that, since he no longer had the confidence of his superiors, he was resigning.

So ended, pensionless and without prospect, his 34 years' service with the Forestry Commission.

His successor was Dallas Mithen (1968–71) who, five years earlier as a district officer, had created his own working plan for the New Forest – although Cadman had allowed him no chance to put it into operation at anything like the speed he had desired. This plan, as well as laying low an inordinate number of broadleaf trees during the short period of its lifetime, was to shake the Commission to its very roots and prove that the environmentalist lobby had a voice and could use it.

Mithen's concept of the Forest's usefulness was clear-cut. It was to produce marketable timber. To that end, unprofitable broadleaves were to be phased out and replaced by quick-growing, fast-selling softwood varieties. By the late 1960s, Hasley, Lower Sloden, Knightwood and Puckpits were badly affected. Inroads were being made at Rushpole and Tantany and Godshill were next in line.

As a concession to the amenity groups, Mithen was holding occasional meetings with a 'consultative committee' of the New Forest Assocation.

David Stagg was a member of this committee, and recalls that its inquiries about the working plan were always left unanswered and that Mithen kept his copy of it locked in a desk drawer.

'He would take it out and pat the cover and then lock it away again,' says Stagg. 'There were times when he left it lying on the desk but we were never allowed to see what was in it.'

In any event, the committee tired of the game. Stagg, who knew a little about Government departments, wrote to the Forestry Commission headquarters at Alice Holt, saying he was interested in the future strategy for the Forest and asking if he might see the working plan. The Commission responded by inviting him up to Alice Holt and offering him any facilities he needed.

When they gave him a quiet room to peruse the document at his leisure, he photographed significant passages, thanked the Commission for their co-operation, came back to the Forest – and in early autumn, 1970, he and Jean Main Cobb blew the works to a sympathetic Press.

For the first time, it could be demonstrated in the Commission's own words that the woodland was to be cropped on a set rotation, a measure that would eliminate nearly all the hardwoods from the inclosures. And such was the volume of public outcry, not just from Forest and fringes but nationwide from people for whom 'environment' was taking on a new meaning (or indeed any kind of meaning) that the then Minister of Agriculture, Mr James Prior, imposed a ban on all hardwood felling in the New Forest until the subject had been reviewed comprehensively.

On May 3, 1971, the Minister attended the Verderers' Court to present a mandate which would form the basis of the New Forest management plan (1972–81). Its major objectives were:

'The New Forest is to be regarded as a national heritage and priority given to the conservation of its traditional character.

'The Ancient and Ornamental Woodlands are to be conserved without regard to timber production objectives.

'In the Statutory Inclosures the existing balance between conifers and broadleaves is to be maintained; the latter are to be managed with greater emphasis on visual amenity, on a rotation of at least 200 years and felling limited to single trees or small groups.'

And that, you might feel (as I do) is the best you have the right to expect in an imperfect world.

Two months prior to this historic announcement had been appointed the man who has put the words into action.

If Donn Small wants to be remembered for anything from his term as Deputy Surveyor, he tells me, let it be for the recreational management.

Though his knowledge of timber is immense – he is equally at home among the pines of the Scottish peaks or the rain forests of the Far East – it wasn't until he took up his Hampshire post that he was faced with the novel problem of ensuring a proper relationship between trees and people. The difficulty is in the paradoxical nature of the task.

He has, for instance, to house more people in fewer places (and the same may be said of their vehicles, domestic or transitory); to make more money with fewer options – there seems to be a hint of suspicion every time anybody mentions cash and Commission in the same sentence, but the fact remains that even a forest has overheads, wages to pay, machinery to maintain and replace.

Since the mandate has put a brake on the type of trees that can be marketed, the deficit must be met by new and diversified uses for timber that *is* saleable.

He has to be a servant of the Crown and a friend to the tenant, not always an easy combination and seldom achieved in old Ytene, where even the most straightforward individual is considered crooked because that is, rightly or wrongly, the tradition.

The management plan takes us up to 1981. Donn Small assures me that no revolution is planned for 1982. Consultative documents which have been released by and through the Commission in the late seventies show that their main concerns are to keep things as they are – things as different as model aircraft and gravel extraction – and to contain the people boom.

But constantly, there are little things happening in the Forest which touch the whole situation with a kind of crazy humour.

Recently, Donn Small received a letter which said, simply: 'Can you do something about the "B", please?' Thoroughly mystified, he got back to his correspondent to seek more details.

The 'B', it transpired, was in 'Beaulieu', the word marked out in stones on an obscure part of the heath, unappreciable from the ground but intended to be a guide for returning wartime flyers.

From some rough directions supplied by the letter-writer, Small sought and found the landmark. The 'B' had been covered by an encroachment of gorse. A Forestry Commission team not only cleared the furze but renewed the stones throughout the word . . . and considered they had made a profit, because they had found out something they didn't know about the Forest.

A grateful letter a little while later from their informant said, in spirit: 'Thank you . . . We don't have too many reminders now of the good old days!'

The Verderers' Court

THE Queen's House, Lyndhurst, within a red-brick shell of mid-17th century construction, encloses the steel and emulsion of modern offices, the smoked and brooding beams of a Georgian conference room, and the authentic discomfort of the Verderers' Court – or the Court of Swainmote and Attachment, as was its ancient title. Here, at least six times a year, on a Monday morning at the stroke of eleven, the Verderers gather to hear the grievances of Forest residents, in what must surely be the most democratic court in the land. The presentments (petitions) come from the high and the humble. The Forestry Commission cannot move in an encompassing way without doing it via the Verderers; the smallholder cannot run one extra animal on the Forest unless he has permission from this Rule of Ten, headed by the Official Verderer, appointed by the Monarch.

On the lighter side of democracy, as you might say, the spectators on these occasions can be almost certain of amusement to go along with their illumination and their stiff haunches. What passes in this court for novelty of approach by a petitioner might be cited as contempt in other, staider arenas.

It is ten minutes before eleven o'clock, and the tall room is filling up.

Conversations and greetings are manifold. It seems more like a congregation than a courtroom. A few seconds short of the hour, a door opens halfway down the right of the room and the Official Verderer enters, accompanied by the four green-clad agisters who are full-time employees of the Verderers. From various parts of the room, individuals break away from chatting groups to take their places on the high bench, facing out over seats which owe a great deal to pews in their design – the sort of pews fashioned to stop you nodding off.

One of the agisters climbs to the witness stand. I use the word 'climb' quite deliberately because it is an ascent on a par with the north face of the Eiger. Any complainant will tell you that once he or she has made it up the woodwork to the top, the mere business of advocacy is an anticlimax.

Then, with right arm aloft, the agister recites:

'OYEZ! OYEZ! OYEZ!

'All manner of persons who have any presentment to make or matter of things to do at this Court of Verderers – let them come forward and they shall be heard. God save the Queen.'

He gives the declaration a fine-sounding ring and then looks decidedly nervous about descending from the stand. The court work is a bit of a bind

Verderer, Hugh Pasmore, chats with a Forester on one of his patrols across the open wastelands.

for these outdoor types – thank goodness it only comes up every six weeks or so – and they would far sooner be about their usual business, pulling ponies from bogs or marking tails and collecting fees and otherwise checking on animal welfare.

For the Verderers themselves, the open session, which seldom lasts more than an hour, is only the outward and visible sign of an inward and invisible machinery that will take up the rest of the day and longer because natural justice is rarely aided by precedent or Stone's Justices' Manual. In fact, it is a wonder that these ordinary humans can so often emulate Solomon in their decisions.

And what will exercise them today? Well, there's a frail-looking lady with the voice of a Bernhardt, citing the state of her village green – the heap of old iron in the centre of the grass and the piles of sand and bricks nearby. If that is acceptable, so be it. What she is seeking is equity. But she has noticed that when a vehicle is parked on the grass, its owner is asked to remove it at once; if a delivery of fuel for the winter is unloaded outside a house, then it must be removed at once.

She hopes she will not be considered just another country crank. She does not become hysterical every time she sees a car parked on the Forest and she does not go into ecstasies over a dragonfly. But she is looking for equity – and if her neighbour can have a pile of rubbish on the village green, then can she have one, too?

This, believe it or not, is her approach to a court of law, and illustrates very well what I have said about democracy. No contempt is occurring here, only an expectation of sympathy and understanding from the administrators – and sufficient ease among the presentment-makers to allow them to be themselves. For certain, this lady would make excellent preserves and write memorable letters to *The Times*.

Her immediate predecessor has been another lady, rather more tweedy, with two complaints – that Forestry Commission tractors at Bartley keep using the same rut so that the grass verge is given no chance to recover; and that 15 ponies in one spot at East Hill are turning the area into a morass.

Earlier, there have been complaints of rubbish – picnic or itinerant – at Ober Water, Emery Down, Millersford Bottom.

A gentleman from Brockenhurst Parish Council has made the point that a shortwave radio mast being erected for Southern Gas at Setley has already outstripped the height for which planning permission has been given. He finds unexpected support from the Forestry Commission – the ubiquitous Donn Small – who says he has observed the same thing. (As it happens, I know, roughly, what happened to that presentment. The New Forest District Council – the planning authority – made their own investigation.

Remedial talks between councillors, Southern Gas and the Post Office later took up a great deal of time.)

And now the Commoners' Defence Association is having a contretemps with the Commission (the Verderers serving as the referee) over the ration of heath to be controlled by fire.

This, described with totally conscious ambiguity as 'the burning question', is a regular feature – and best explains the kind of situation that exists chronically between the Forest's three controlling bodies. There are no villains, but it goes like this: the Forestry Commission will be watched closely as long as the Verderers hold their courts and as long as the Commoners have an axe to grind or a ditch to clear: the Verderers themselves will be cited by the Crown for obstruction or accused by the Commoners of apathy or self-interest: and the Commoners will be fingered by the Commission for high-handedness and suspected by the Verderers of certain activities which approach the format of the rural guerrilla.

(But an evidence that these differences – triangular as often as two-sided – should not be taken too seriously in this day and age is that the Crown and the Verderers' Court occupy opposite ends of the Queen's House without, apparently, injury, explosion or loss of face.)

To return to the progress of the burning question. In the witness stand the man from the Commoners' Defence Association has all his points written

Queen's House, Lyndhurst, houses the Forestry Commission at the near end and the Verderer's Court at the far end.

down to ensure that he forgets nothing, but you still form the distinct impression that there have been any number of these performances over the years, and not just one to a year.

He quotes a former Deputy Surveyor, David Young, writing in the Forestry Commission guide reprinted in 1966 of 'The Forester's Task'. There, he says, Mr Young has outlined an annual target of 2,500 acres for clearance of coarse vegetation. Between 1972 and 1975, he says, the Forestry Commission cleared a total of 850 acres. In 1976–77, they managed 331 acres and he wonders if they have been making the maximum effort. He hopes that their 1977–78 figure will be rather more satisfactory. (In fact, it was very much the same sort of figure.)

Donn Small, replying via the Bench, says there is a difference between paper targets and realities, and submits, with suitable humility, that the Commission cannot be held responsible for the weather.

The issue is a slow burner. It has been smouldering for decades and it is one, at least, on which the Verderers will not have to rule. Just as well. The search for equity at that level would be beyond any giant of the judiciary.

But on one village green, before very long, a take-your-time developer is going to be asked to move his materials before everybody joins in.

And that's justice.

Rhinefield Walk

THIS is the tale of a conversion. Moscow had given us a May Day holiday and the heavens had given us Wood Fidley rain and we went, on a whim, to Rhinefield. And there, as you will see, I came to appreciate conifers.

Our first attempt to enter from the Brockenhurst end of the ornamental drive was thwarted by flooding. The watersplash, normally barely enough of a presence to dampen the tyres, was now overlapping the roads in all directions and only fools and Land-Rovers were attempting passage. So we retraced our tracks across Hinchelsea Moor, past the Naked Man tree at Wilverly – called thus, it was once insisted, because the naked body of highwayman Mark Way was gibbeted here; in fact, 'Mark Way' was merely a fantasising of the old Marked Way road and the tree gained its name purely on the basis of appearance – and back onto the Christchurch-Lyndhurst road at the Holmsley Tea Rooms where business, to judge from the parked cars, was far better than the weather might suggest.

The tea rooms occupy the old station house. Not too many years ago, this was as close as the railway came to Bournemouth before pressing on through Ringwood to Dorchester and leaving seaward travellers to cover the last 12 miles by coach and horses. Prior to steam, Sir Walter Scott used to favour this undulating area of moorland between Holmsley and Burley as he did no other Southern stretch because it reminded him best of his Scottish homeland.

At Holmsley, then, we rejoined the main road and suffered no more impediment, although low-lying woodland to either side was giving eloquent evidence of the everglades the Forest could have become but for the introduction of something approaching adequate drainage.

Into Rhinefield and out of the car at Brock Hill.

The dips in the chalk paths of Tall Trees Walk were filling up, but puddles are a pleasure to the gumboot, as any child will tell you – and any adult who can be that honest with himself. In fact, the whole concept of rain has been incentive rather than deterrent to my little family for as long as we can remember. It is a minority choice – but some of our most memorable walks have been taken when the clouds looked low enough to touch and the rest of the world seemed to have been washed away.

Rhinefield, of course, is predominantly conifer – a showcase of softwood varieties. I have already stated my prejudice against these shifty, mercenary intruders, fast-growing, freakish and not above giving you an unseasonal

Rhinefield House was built at the end of the 19th century in the style of the Stuarts.

chill. (It is, I should add, a conviction my wife never shared.) But here, given the common factor of the downpour and an illumination that was the same inside the stands as outside them, the whole plantation began to present itself to me in a new way.

Before me was a genuine raindrop tree – an oak, stunted by close and hostile companionship, not yet showing bud or leaf but made glorious in foliage by the minute silver globules aligned along its branches. And a foliage blessed with miraculous replacement. When I did the autumn job to a low twig by shaking it, more drops trickled out from the trunk and formed themselves up like a chorus line to bring it back to spring.

From there, I was suddenly taking note of the number of broadleaves that existed alongside fir and hemlock, spruce and redwood. There were beeches with a green mist about their upper boughs, silver birch exchanging the last of their previous year's gold coins for new, pale currency, stands of oak reluctant to express the season while the rust still tinted the ground at their toes. Growth was hesitant in this cold, wet spring but it was there and I had been less than just for overlooking it.

We left the path and headed into a thicket of pine towards a central area where some of the giants were down and showing us their roots. Four had fallen in a rough kind of line like dominoes. I scanned the area for tracks which would have indicated some manual participation in the event but the woodland floor was undisturbed.

It is difficult to know why one tree, shielded on every side by its fellows, should suddenly feel the need to end its upward aspirations – but one tree is all it takes, one tree and the ninepin principle . . . the first tree pushes over a second and their combined weight takes out a third and so on until the way is clear for a wholesale downfall. A lay examination of the roots and the shallow depression which has unleashed them gives some idea of the ease with which these accidents can happen – and explains, perhaps why quantity should play as large a part as quality in the Forestry Commission's planting strategy. But that first failing – that remains the mystery.

The mishap is not a complete loss. The Commission will still utilise the timber – and the ground beneath will benefit from the space opened up in the canopy. While the trunks stood firm, there was little to note on the thicket floor except the mudpack of needles and the occasional stump. But here, where the sky had been allowed to intervene – and daylight is the magic ingredient, not sunlight; plant growth requires only very little candlepower – the Forest was back in business with a vengeance.

Ferns, determined to succeed, were uncurling among shed branches and flaked bark. Tongue-like leaves promised a foxglove. And already, the generation to replace this fallen generation was gaining stature.

The feeling is strange. You may enjoy a puppy because he is a miniature version of his parent. You may love a baby because of his perfection of detail. And somewhere, in that same family of emotions you develop an admiration for this . . . frond, this pale-green upstart with paler puffs like thistledown at the ends of its meagre arms. You almost wish you could dig it up and take it home to nurture but that, of course, is a major violation of Forest and natural law.

The day taketh away; the day giveth. A high wind may have sent this shrub's tall ancestor on its downward course – and in so doing has torn a hole in the lowering ceiling that was holding this young fellow back from life. That is justice, conifer-style.

Circuitously, we were back on the ride dominated by two California redwoods, dwarves and infants by Big Sur standards but tall enough to take pride of place in this Western European walk. Before us and behind us, grey squirrels flickered across the ride on urgent business. On such missions, they are the very model of caution, moving in fits and starts, freezing when they feel the weight of a gaze (and make no mistake, attention is like avoirdupois with them), putting the width of a tree-trunk between them and their observers but without an accurate regard for their own size, so that very often a nose tip or a whisker of tail will give them away. Ostrich-like, they reason that if they can't see you, you can't see them.

But that very morning, I had seen a squirrel, acting as though unobserved, quite literally take his (or it could have been her) life in his paws.

Our breakfast room window looks out upon an avenue of Corsican pine. Branch tips come within about six feet of each other at the closest point. So here went the squirrel, swarming up one trunk and considering a mid-air transfer, though why he had not chosen to scale the neighbouring tree at the outset is something mere humans cannot discern.

The first branch he tried ran out of wood a long way short of its counter part. The next branch up was longer, stronger and took him closer to his goal but was still something like a dozen squirrel-lengths away. He advanced along the branch, thought about it and turned back, rethought and advanced, reconsidered and went back.

And then, while the three of us watched with bated breath, he pushed doubt to one side, picked up speed along the dipping branch and launched himself into the void. He had to fall, we thought. Even if he covered the distance, the slim twiglets at the end of the target branch would never hold his weight. We pictured the small grey body dropping like a stone.

But somehow, with a cling and a wriggle, he was aboard the new tree and away as though nothing untoward had taken place – while we wiped our

Rhinefield Walk – a bridge over the Blackwater, which changes from idling stream to swift channel in rainy weather.

brows and waited for our hearts to stop pounding. Allowing for the thickness of twig he had required for a solid launch and the sturdiness of branch he had needed for a safe landing, his leap must have covered around twelve feet.

If caution had been a permanent principle, our small friend would have settled for a quick and entirely safe shuttle through the underbrush and then a conservative climb up the neighbouring trunk. But it seems the squirrel, left to his own devices, prefers the daredevil way. Even so, it was almost a comfort that afternoon to see that his brothers were sticking to the ground.

We took the bridge over the Blackwater, and as it passed beneath our feet we heard its throaty chuckle. Usually, the drainage channels that mark its course through this part of the Forest are dry enough to be used as hiding-places for small children who flicker ahead of their families like squirrels, their parents turning Billy Goat Gruff as they stump across the wooden bridges, matching shock for shock with the offspring whose presence they are not supposed to suspect.

But today all channels were full and flowing and the walk had developed an almost Venetian punctuation.

Flowing water has a fascination for me. The narrower the stream, the lumpier the bed, the happier I am. Still water gives no comfort. It merely reflects its surroundings and a mirror is useless when you are looking for a friend. But the silver runner is therapeutic. Follow its path and it soothes the eye; hear its chatter and you are immersed in good-sounding conversation; submit to its strength of purpose and you feel your own weariness draining away through the soles of your feet.

Deep thoughts above deep water. The torrent chuckles at your serious face and cheers you with a reminder of the mayhem it is working downstream with its companions, Highland and old Ober – at Brockenhurst, where their confluent excesses are already a police matter.

The titmice bang their vocal anvils and blow forth their sparks of song, the low-toned bullfinches shelter with their collars turned up under the budding azaleas and the tiniest brown wren, the one leaf on a bare branch, watches us on our way. We are happy – happy as those who expect to find wonder and are not disappointed. Happy in the rain.

Flora

THE largest flowers in the Forest are the trees themselves, and even though stands may have been shunted around over the years, the actual variety of display today is not a great deal removed from the original. Then, as now, we would have had two types of oak, sessile and pedunculate, beeches, birches and alder along the streamsides. To a lesser degree, there would have been ash, willow, aspen poplar, yew, crab apple, hawthorn, blackthorn, field maple, alder buckthorn and holly.

Limes would have been native, too – 'Lyndhurst' means 'inclosed field by the lime or linden trees' – but since livestock enjoys lime saplings, one might say with some justification that that part of the Forest had been eaten.

The same may well be true of any elms which the old Forest harboured, and if so they were mercifully spared the contemporary attention of the fungus Ceratosystis ulmi and the elm bark beetle, the deadly combination which together make Dutch elm disease. (Elms were plentiful along the bordering Avon Valley, and now their one-time abundance is underlined mournfully by the extent of their absence and by the winter barrenness which dogs so many summer skylines in Southern Britain.)

Scots pine, reintroduced fairly recently, was also here at the outset but was probably wiped out by its flammability – either in heath fires or at local hearths. Similarly, juniper, which still survives on the downs north of the Forest.

Crab apple has a way of sticking to the older parts of the Forest, which gives it a kind of authority in woodland affairs, and its fruits in late summer – when you can find a strain that is fruiting – makes the most delicious jelly or preserve. Blackthorn has something of the same manner and the search for sloes is described at length in a little while.

But I want to say a word for a scrubland tree which rather took us by surprise this year (1978) – the elder.

In recent springs, when we have been seeking out the delicate, multi-faceted elderflower for champagne – eight heads will make a gallon and no tree will notice the loss – the growths were so rare that we had to make a mental note of locations. This year, they were everywhere, and sizeable, too. They must have been lurking in hedgerows, unblossoming until some coincidental feature of the climate, some consideration of age or growth brought a jubilee.

The father of the Forest is the oak, and because the ground layer presents two soils – basic (alkaline) and acid – there are good examples of both main kinds, the pedunculate and the sessile. 'Pedunculate' is a mouthful of a word, but we are stuck with it. The two alternatives, 'common' or 'English', are not accurate because there are areas where this particular family of oak is not at all common (whereas the sessile is) and, by the same reasoning, the pedunculate is no more 'English' than its cousin.

There are simple ways of defining the two types but you have to be close-up to see them. The acorns of the pedunculate are mounted on small stalks known as peduncles (hence the name) and the leaves are short-stemmed with a little curl (auricle) at the base; while 'sessile' comes from the Latin word for 'seated' and the sessile acorns clamp close to the branch whose leaves have a longish stalk and no auricle.

Examination of the two leaves reveals other differences in general shape, hairiness, lobing, colour and texture. Bark, buds and shape of tree are also distinctive. One key factor which has geographical as well as ecological importance is that the pedunculate favours a deepish, loamy soil while a sessile can thrive quite happily on the shallow, acid soil one may find on Forest hillsides. Look at the ground and you may well be able to guess the identity of the gnarled old fellow who is giving you shade.

The way the oak can drape itself about, or the way pollarding has left it – the Knightwood Oak at Bolderwood is a good example of this – can make it a piece of sculpture in itself, and my own tree preferences may be governed by my priorities in art.

Though I can be moved by the voice that speaks from the stone or the

A venerable representative of ancient hardwood.

alabaster, the impact is more immediate (and more frequent) from the message on canvas. I can enjoy looking at paintings, good or bad, ancient or modern, for hours. My predilection for beeches, therefore, may well be as much to do with the way the spring colour dusts their upper branches or the way the sunbeams slot through them as it is to do with their individual beauty of form. My Forest, I suppose, is the Forest of Lucy Kemp-Welch, Golden Short, E.W. Haslehust and Walter Tyndale. But to be fair and contradictory at the same time, the modern Forest artist whose work moves me most is wood carver Ron Lane, of Waterside, and his unexpected death in 1976 gives an added poignancy to the carven creatures who survive him.

It is an inadequacy to describe autumn among the trees as 'Fall'. The process is rather more intricate than that, and I sat in Bolderwood one magnificent late October while my wife and son produced marvellous sketches and tried to paint my picture in this way:

The beeches barely make a stand
Before the autumn hold-up man.
Like ladies, to remain discreet,
They cast their jewels at his feet.

The silver birches, no more bold,
Dissolve into a shower of gold.
They know the villain won't think twice
Before he touches them with ice.

The chestnut has no chance to rust,
Too soon its leaves have come to dust.
The oak is sly – he sees at first
If acorns will deter the worst.

Then he surrenders, leaf by leaf,
He tries the patience of the thief,
Now green, now yellow edged with brown.
Late in the day, his coins drift down.

At last, the scoundrel overwhelms
The preparations of the elms –
And will his only failure be
The resolute azalea tree?

When trees stand naked to the cold,
When foliage is reduced to mould,
Then elm-bud, safe beneath its plate,
Becomes the devil's advocate.

The desperado of the wood
Is miscast in the role of hood.
Without him and without the fall,
There could not be a spring at all . . .

You will note I make little attempt to describe the evergreens and conifers – not because of my previously mentioned bias which, by now, has been 90 per cent dispelled – but because they are better illustrated than described. Ramble through Rhinefield, as we did, and you may understand my difficulty.

But one evergreen inhabitant must bear the burden of my faltering expertise and that is the rhododendron. I do not know who introduced rhododendron and azalea to the Forest – I doubt if anybody does – but I know they have been cursed since by foresters who consider the May/June spectacle no better than a creeper.

To me, it is nearer an orchid. Why people can take a special trip to look at regimented fields of tulips and yet not venture down their nearest Forest lane to enjoy the local masterpiece, I cannot understand. The two ornamental drives – Rhinefield, in particular – are supposed to provide the best examples of these mountainous blooms, but my own choice would be the backroad from Christchurch to Ringwood, via Bransgore, which takes you through Ripley Wood. Along the main road, too (B3347), there are flashing glimpses of high banks of flowers and the Christchurch-Lyndhurst road (A35) has its share.

Flowers are largely governed by the trees which surround them and the amount of leeway they are allowed as a result, so that they may be profuse where the canopy is mixed or broken and cowed and weakly where thick foliage limits the fall of ultra-violet.

Oak woods on rich soil would be the ideal choice for dog's mercury, bugle, primrose, yellow archangel, wood sanicle, wood spotted orchis, early purple orchis, enchanter's nightshade, wild strawberry, wood anemone, red campion and herb Robert. The latter three might also be found on the acid soil, but not in the same quantity. More likely companions to the sessile oak are bluebells, wood sorrel, foxglove, upright St John's wort, cow-wheat, heath bedstraw, tormentil and golden rod.

The flora beneath healthy beeches tend to be undramatic because the trees' autumn deposit of leaves runs deep and rots slowly. The few flowers that thrive do so by early-spring blossoming, before shade gets too dense, or by special adaptations – like the yellow birdsnest, a plant which is more of a fungus because it does not need photosynthesis, feeding instead on decaying matter. By this means, the saprophytic birdsnest manages to make its appearance in July and August when the leaf cover is at its thickest.

There is a possibility of the birdsnest orchid, also a saprophyte, flowering in June or July. The same dense cover provides an incentive for fungi – toadstools of the *Russula* and Amanita family and brackets like the beech tuft, *Ganoderma applanatum* and *Hericium caralloides*.

Ornamental drive near Brockenhurst – in May and June, rhododendrons provide a footstool for the giant pines.

Where the canopy is fitful, the flowers on view are those common to lime-rich soils, bluebell, wood sorrel, upright St John's wort and the rest.

The ground layer around and beneath conifers changes as they grow. When they are young, grasses, heather, bilberry, crowberry, gorse can all live alongside. But as their increasing stature permits less and less light to filter to earth, so the fall of needles blanks out much of the activity until the ground is left to fern, foxglove and fungus.

The floral gems of the Forest are to be found well clear of the trees – so that time and daylight might preclude you from enjoying both fortunes at the same time. No matter. One visit is never enough.

I have mentioned the gorse and heather which gain their radiance when the sky loses its own, but, on the moorland areas, the botanist may be just as interested in their parasite, the dodder, whose thread-like red stems and clusters of whitish flowers play the spider's web both horizontally (heather) and vertically (gorse). In the higher moorlands, most plants find the gravel topping a hard way to make a living but ragwort persists and, in summer and autumn, the roadsides boast hawkbit and other yellow composites of the *Leontodon* genus. On the lower heathlands, however, the other extreme is reached – and the nibbling ponies certainly do not deter such verge regulars as the pale heath violet (spring), the common centaury (summer and autumn). The well-grazed turf also attracts eyebrights of the *nemorosa* and *angelica* groups.

The heath spotted orchid enjoys the acid soils and grows in large colonies where the ground is fairly dry. It differs from the other spotted orchid, found in a more wooded habitat, by the shape of its lower leaves, by shape of bloom and colouring. The Forest rather specialises in orchids and they can be found in wet or dry, dark or light surroundings. The early purple orchid, as likely to be found on roadside grass as at the edge of a copse, has no appetite for acid soil and that makes it a rarity in the Forest proper. The fragrant orchid is another occasional resident but the lesser butterfly orchid is not at all fussy, with its range taking in dry, bracken-covered slopes and very wet bogs.

The broad helleborine likes grass verges under trees and there was a time when the marsh helleborine was in evidence at one point until – believes local botanist Brigadier F.E. Venning – the laying of a pipeline dispatched it. The twayblade, which also effects a liking for wet copses and woodlands, remains plentiful.

Something of an enigma is the autumn lady's tresses, which can make regular appearances at the same location for several years and then disappear – only to poke up again when you have decided it has gone for good. Gone for definite, however, is the summer lady's tresses, which was unique to the New Forest and at one time fairly abundant in marshy places. Its numbers dwindled from about 200 spikes counted to twenty and then to six. For a good many years, according to a 1966 observation, it had not been seen and was feared extinct – unless it was adopting the same Pimpernel tactics as its autumn cousins.

The milkwort is to be seen from late spring and through the summer where the heather is not too thick and most of the speedwells are also in attendance. Creeping species on the open heath include the heath bedstraw (late summer) and lady's bedstraw. The great hedge bedstraw and the goose grass find their way into the hedgerows. The wild madder is rare, the field madder does not climb at all and the related sweet woodruff is a curiosity with a preference for calcareous soils under Forest trees. Sheep's bit scabious and devil's bit scabious, similar in appearance, can be distinguished by their habitats – devil's bit prefers damper areas. I have a liking also for the hare's tail cotton grass (spring/early summer) which waves its flags across the sphagnum moors between Crow and Burley Street and Burley and Holmsley. Ponies wandering among the dramatic gestures seem to have strayed into some boggy Lilliput.

The special soil circumstances ensure that the Forest has certain small rations of ferns better known in the West Country – maidenhair spleenwort, rusty-back and harts-tongue.

Damp ground provides the flower-watcher with his greatest prizes – like the striking golden-yellow bog asphodel (late summer), and marsh gentian (autumn) and the marsh St John's wort, while Forest ponds accommodate several types of burweed, water-lilies, the spearwort and one plant known only in the New Forest and Jersey, the *Ludwigia palustris*, from the willow-herb family. Along the shores of the ponds are the local carnivores – round-leaved and long-leaved sundew and the rarer great sundew, pale butterwort and lesser bladderwort. The keen eye will also pick out bog orchid, brown beak-sedge, yellow balsam and water forget-me-not.

But the guideline, if one exists for an area of so many and varied habitats as the New Forest, is to keep your eyes open and your reference book handy because what you see may surprise you – and could even surprise the experts.

Blackberry Capital

CALL September the month of the tin. Many people in this age of packed-up freshness favour the Polythene bag, but I can never understand why – there is nothing like condensation for putting a fur on the fruit-pile.

I am talking about blackberries – and about a bramble jelly that never fails to release the essence of a Forest autumn on to our bread and into our midst the whole year round.

Come September, the roadside ponies are not the only hedge-croppers. People join them – with hooks and crooks of marvellous ingenuity. In the winding lanes between Emery Down and Minstead, on scrubland at Oakley South, Canterton, Wootton and at the back of Burley Lodge, the tares and dog roses are ravished for the berries that lie amongst them. But not by me. When I want blackberries, I go to the capital – why settle for anything less? And although the secret becomes more open with every passing autumn, this remains a focal centre uncelebrated by sign or direction.

It is not where you would think it to be. Passing it by along the two roads which border it – Bransgore to Burley and Holmsley to Avon Tyrrell – you would not suspect anything more sacred than a tangled wasteland populated by oaks that haven't quite made it and hollies and sloes that have made it only too well.

But you would underestimate it. Here, the battle between holly and bramble has been hand to hand and rages still, with the outcome changing from year to year – even, you suspect, from day to day. If you lose in the autumn, you gain in the winter because where the blackberries fail, the red berries triumph. Jam for the cupboard or colour for the Christmas cornice.

This fall, the brambles were winning. We came back in all weathers, but the rain was the most fun. Gumbooted and mackintoshed, with absurd hats and scarves about our heads, we braved the crystal showers dislodged as we plunged, fearless, into thickets, marking our hands but filling our vessels until they ran over. (You cannot take blackberries with gloves on, and after the first couple of twinges the prickles count less with you than the rewards.) So we picked – and unpicked – our way between the glades, discovering as we went that the sky had dried up even though the drizzle continued beneath the boughs.

If the fruits you seek are neither black nor red but a dusty blue which polishes to purple at the touch of your finger, then take a little more care. The first sloe is the toughest. Though the berry is distinctive; though its foliage is sparse; though its branches are few enough to be far between, still it manages a kind of camouflage that will evade the casual stroller. But find one sloe for your gin and your eyes move naturally to another and another and another until you are breathless with the maroon harvest which you so nearly missed. The protective barbs, by the way, are longer and sharper than brambles but less of a hazard because they have not the same talent for entanglement.

Moving northward from the juicy strongholds towards Burley, we found copses giving way to clumps and clumps being succeeded by furze bushes. The horizon was but a short way hence, lined with high furze and the bronze skeletons of fern; then suddenly the terrain had dropped away in a basin, rising again at distant Burley. More of a saucer than a basin, in fact, and a cracked one, at that; the cracks silvered like a dewy web and all spidering in towards a pond glinting under the overcast sky.

You can try finding footholds among the wedges of heather and dodder which pass for dry land in this delta, but it is far more satisfying to accept and enjoy the inevitable and spend as much of your time paddling the rivulets as pounding the peat.

Besides, you are walking on a vision. Juliette de Bairacli Levy said of her beloved 'Windmill Pond': 'The entire base . . . being grass, it is possible, when the rains have given the water sufficient depth, to swim there slowly and gaze down upon flowers like mer-things shining at the bottom, especially the white daisy-like camomile with the golden pin-cushion centres and the square-form blossoms of cinquefoil amongst its silver fern-like leaves. And all that stretch of water, being of the rains, is like silk upon our bodies. What worries and troubles those waters have taken away from me . . .'

While we walked upon the waters of Holmsley Plain, we made our own interpretation of the vision. For there, in the stream beds, bending to the will of the water, bell heather and ling entered a submarine existence while grass was brushed back like hair.

Still ankle-deep in this discovery, we chanced to lift our eyes to the pool and found that closeness had lent enchantment.

Throughout our stroll, we had come upon furze bushes that turned out to be ponies and ponies that turned out to be furze bushes, but here was something of which we had been given no hint. On a stretch of shore so green that it startled among so many shades of brown, hunched shapes thrust out necks, wings, webbed feet and turned to scan us with clown faces ringed in white. They were Canada geese, five in all, not perturbed by our approach but ruling that a little water between us and them would be no bad thing.

The same launching movement that showed them clumsy upon land rendered them graceful upon the pool – and the fleet of mallard who had been tacking back and forth had already taken flight in the space of one thought, banking eastward to another pond beyond our vision, strung out in a formation that would have glorified a cathedral window, let alone a living-room wall.

Surrounded by wonders, it is easy to be greedy. But the dusk put a brake on our appetites that day. The sun, which had spent the waning afternoon skulking behind Alpine ranges of cloud, suddenly reappeared above the coniferous skyline of Dur Wood, gave us five minutes of red-orange farewell and then dropped like a stone, leaving all purple in its wake.

The rivulets were apparent by the way they caught the dwindling light, although there was nothing to choose for colour. Fortunately, a way lay straight and short to the road.

As we climbed back towards the blackberries, the rain came swishing across the stage in a final curtain.

The Pony Factory

RIDDEN or unridden, groomed to a nicety or shaggy as a rug, the pony is almost certainly the first animal you will see in the Forest – except perhaps in the north, where the donkeys of Godshill, Blissford and Frogham may intervene.

Juliette de Bairacli Levy, whose book *Wanderers in the New Forest* is the most lyrical, if not the most detailed, of Forest literature, had a Commoner friend who had seen deer frisking with ponies; but one needs no special insight to see ponies frisking alone.

Sometimes they have very little reason to frisk. In a wet spring they can endure the discomfort of rain rash, and that is best understood in the appearance of wobbly foals who are cute down to their long eyelashes but bear splotchy disfigurements on their coats. In a dry summer, the pony can be desperate for water, and in the autumnal acorn boom which so often follows such a drought (like 1976) the animal will eat its fill of the delicious mast beneath the trees and then know only pain and perplexity as its feast kills it.

At the best of times, the pony has to graze all day and well into the night, not from greed but from necessity. One reason for this present hunger is the cross-breeding which has tinkered with many of the traditional failsafes in pursuit of a model that will suit the changing market – failsafes like whiskers, a hardy diet and a rough palate.

Elizabeth Godfrey, writing of the gypsy child forced to enter a formal environment, could equally well have been describing the pony – that Forest creature closest in spirit to the Romany and echoing his history over roughly the same period. The young gypsy, she wrote, 'goes in sharp as a needle, cunning as a fox, sagacious with ancient woodland lore; he comes out stupid, blear-eyed . . . liable to colds and ailments hitherto unknown . . .'

But while the gypsies have gone from the Forest, the pony remains – such as he is; or rather, such as *she* is because it is the female of the species who has carried the can all these years.

The original New Forest pony, native by shape or even by temperament, is so far gone now that we can only theorise – and one of the fairly popular theories, at least, can soon be dismissed.

It is said that the breed was largely influenced by Spanish stallions who emerged dripping from the Solent when the Armada had been scuttled. Wise quotes this with some cynicism. Horace Hutchinson's *The New Forest*

Donkeys on the northern edge of the Forest.

(first edition, 1906) applies the belief to donkeys and not ponies – although the arrival of any animal immigrants at all by this means needs a lot of confirmation.

Pam Harvey Richards, whose involvement with the pony fraternity is only rivalled by her attention to comfort at her pub, the Green Dragon at Brook (where, incidentally, you can get the best ham sandwiches in the Forest), takes the equine origins right back to the days when landscape was still largely a matter of plate tectonics.

Then, Britain and Northern Europe were joined by a landbridge and it was across this bridge that the first 'Forest' ponies came tripping.

This conviction finds unconscious support from the observation of Brian Vesey-Fitzgerald that 'shaggy and small, this native breed had more in common with the Kalmuch and Tartar ponies than with southern breeds.'

The first thousand years after Christ are still in the realms of supposition as far as local horse history goes. What is known is that the Southampton area was and had been for centuries a gateway between Britain and the rest of the world. People came but, more importantly, people went, and since the handiest land vehicle of the time became only an extra mouth to feed once it forsook shore for sea, it was very often left behind – either abandoned, in which case it found its own way to the Ytene pasturage or was bought for a song by dealers and then fed for even less on the inherent grazing. In this way, several strains were already at work in the Forest when the ponies were getting their first fleeting mentions in the Forest charters of Canute and the Conqueror.

In 1208, eighteen Welsh mares were introduced and there were sporadic and ill-recorded attempts to 'improve' existing stock. In 1224, the Statute of the Drift of the Forest sought to ensure that poor specimens brought in on the annual round-up were put down.

About 1540, Henry VIII wanted an end to all horses under 14 hands, but the Forest reaction to that was a lack of competence or a lack of enthusiasm or both – a combination repeated 300 years later when Queen Victoria had been talked into outlawing the deer because of their 'devastating' effect on timber production. That same Great Lady probably thought, the following year, that she was making some kind of recompense to Forest fauna when she allowed her Arab stallion, Zorah, to stand at New Park, Brockenhurst, with the idea of introducing some TB (thoroughbred) characteristics into the local herd.

It was a rather naïve assessment of requirements. Zorah never ran out on the Forest and covered only 112 selected mares in the four years of his occupation, and his effect on bloodstock would have been marginal if we were talking solely of performance.

Pam Harvey Richards renews the family brand on one of the leather display panels which show about 300 of the 1,000-odd Commoners' markings at the Green Dragon, Brook.

But the real impact was in the illustrious precedent so established. Because Queen Victoria had done it, suddenly everybody thought it was a good idea and the offers of imports came thick and fast. In 1885, Forest officials hired four well-bred stallions to be used on Commoners' mares, and in 1889 the Queen gave the bandwagon another push with two more Arab stallions, Abegan and Yirassau. Not all bloodlines had been so impeccable. In efforts to produce a pony suitable for the demands that were being made at the time – for draught animals – carthorse and hackney had been tried.

The effect upon the Forest mares themselves – who have never wanted more than to be left to their own devices, which are hazardous enough, goodness knows – must have been traumatic. Certainly, their behaviour changed. They lost the moorland placidity and did not gain the mettlesomeness of the TB Arab. Instead, there was just a nervousness. And that was only the psychological side.

Their appearance, too, was different. Relatively speaking, they were better-looking. In 1784, William Gilpin, Vicar of Boldre, had stated in his *Remarks on Forest Scenery*; 'Their claim to high lineage must in general rest more on their good qualities than on their beauty – on the hardiness of their character – on their uncommon strength – on their agility and sureness of foot, which they probably acquire by constantly lifting their legs among the furze.'

A generation of experiment made them taller, lighter, spindlier and weaker. What was lost in the flesh was not being gained in the bone – and, worse still, the survival traits were being bred out altogether.

In a determined effort to stop the rot, Lord Arthur Cecil, from 1893, began to introduce stallions from sturdy 'local' breeds – Rhums, Fells, Dales, Highlands, Dartmoors and Exmoors. Later, he was joined in his venture by Lord Lucas and the Blackmores of Brockenhurst, and in the New Forest Studbook of 1913 he was able to report: 'It is my belief that sufficient new blood has been brought into the Forest for many years to come. We have had Arabs, Barbs, Thoroughbreds, Dartmoor, Fell and Highland blood and yet, owing to the mysterious power of nature to grind down and assimilate all these types to the one most suited to the land, our breed of Forester is still fairly of one type, and is rapidly becoming more so, and will continue to develop on these lines if the lessons learnt from registration are attended to . . .'

It would be nice to think that some remedy had been found; that some list of priorities might now be drawn up which considered the horse rather than its likely uses. But World War 1 intervened, with its need for expendable flesh with functions dutiful and dubious. The slack years which followed brought the profit motive uppermost again.

A strong revival of equestrianism in the late 1920s and early 1930s increased the demand for Foresters – *not* to trot in front of smart dog-carts but in the secondary role of replacement for the purer breeds which were now no longer available for colliery working and other industrial haulage.

World War 2 took its toll, and the supply-and-demand syndrome has not changed a great deal in the time since. The biggest home requirement is for a child's riding pony and it comes from the modern-day successors to that section which Vesey-Fitzgerald blamed for all Forest deterioration – those people he called, with venom, the 'new middle-class'. But even his well-sustained dislike for the *nouveau riche* might warm to something approaching affection when he compared their role to that of the latest innovation – the EEC buyer.

To my mind, the New Forest pony has little enough to celebrate without reckoning with the gentlemen of Flanders.

See a little herd grazing among the white, fluffy flowers of hare's tail cotton grass in June, the long-legged juniors cavorting with each other or nuzzling up to mother or laid out to nap in the warm mid-day hours, and you might think these are lives into which very little rain could fall. For you, ignorance is bliss. For them, bliss is ignorance.

It is ironic that, just when their appearance is finishing the tricky course from ungainly hybrid to equine beauty, that appearance should begin to matter little or not at all; just when they seem, in general, to be regaining the hardiness and shaking off the Auschwitz variations, their ability to survive should cease to be an important selling factor.

You catch sight of them among the furze, chewing the leguminous tops – gorse is of the pea family – and tenderising the tougher sprigs with their hooves; you see for yourself that the anxieties over the 'soft palate' are out of date even if they were ever fully justified, and you wonder: For what?

You have come up against tradition – and traditionally, the New Forest pony goes to the highest bidder.

There is a phrase in the Forest, used by those charged with deer welfare (and tree welfare), to describe public antagonism to deer-culling. They call it 'the Bambi syndrome'. I don't know if they have a name for being concerned about ponies; but I confess unashamedly to suffering from the Skewbald effect. In identifying it thus, I pay tribute to A.W. Seaby, whose *Skewbald, the New Forest Pony* and *Sons of Skewbald* provide in fictional terms a far more realistic account of the pony's lot than later supposedly scholarly works.

If you can find the books, read them – and you may understand why my family's delight at the sight of a gangling foal is always tempered by a slight moistness of the eye. But even Seaby didn't reckon on the man from Europe.

Pam Harvey Richards makes this point for the breeders: 'To feed a pony costs about £100 in the first year and progressively more as he gets older. You cannot work him until he is four years old, at least, and by that time you have invested something like £500 to £600 in him. What parent is going to pay money like that for something which could turn out to be just a glorified pet? And what vendor is going deliberately to lose money he has already spent by not selling to the highest bidder? It is just unfortunate if the buyer turns out to be a butcher.

'When you rely on horses for your livelihood, you simply cannot afford to be too sentimental. After all, people eat cows and calves, sheep and lambs without quibbling. What's the difference?'

Pam considers the British revulsion for horseflesh to be psychological. We are, she says, descended from races who used to worship the horse and would never stoop to eating their gods. But on the Continent, where spiritual evolution was rather different, there are no such hang-ups.

The Beaulieu Road Sales – held once in April and five times in the autumn – are models of health and hygiene, and the New Forest Pony and Cattle

Beaulieu Road sale: healthy, hygienic . . . and the end of the line for many ponies.

Breeders' Society are proud to have anybody go along and inspect the merchandise for any sign of discomfort. I am quite prepared to accept their assurances – as long as I don't have to go near the sales myself. Well run, they may be – but those air-conditioned juggernauts standing by to carry off some more of our contributions to Europe would disconcert me. And so would the spectacle of mares heavy with foal tripping daintily up the tailboard so that the unborn can make a delicacy on some Flemish dinner-table.

There is a great deal of feeling about the conditions in which livestock are shipped across the Channel. Bournemouth East M.P., Mr David Atkinson, and New Forest M.P., Mr Patrick McNair-Wilson have sought their own assurances from the Ministry that there is no unnecessary suffering (how is *necessary* suffering assessed?) in transit, and the International League for the Protection of Horses, in mid-1978, were promising a closer inspection of conditions and facilities on the French side of the water. The pony, it is stressed, will be given nothing but the best right up to the point of eclipse – and for that, one supposes, a pregnant mare should be grateful . . .

What separates us from the rest of the animals, I think, is the sophistication of our hypocrisy. It gives us the edge in so many ways.

I am not saying that creatures bound for destruction should not be given an easy passage. I am asking, Is their journey really necessary? Bearing in mind the distinct possibility that the Forest could be heading for an actual shortage of ponies – for reasons which I will outline in the concluding chapter – is it wise in the long-term to write them off the Forest and on to the menu?

The matter of finance is tricky when it could be argued that saving a pony could starve a Commoner's child. But if the Ministry of Agriculture can provide a farmer with a cash incentive for not growing a particular crop, then something might surely be arranged to make sure the New Forest keeps its little lawn-mowers.

The Rest of the Fauna

MULTI-STOREY living accommodation, with summer and winter lettings – that is the Forest to the birds which live, and visit, there. The ground floor, in ecological terms, is the ground layer, tenanted by mosses and fungi, seedlings on the way up, leaves on the way down. The first floor is the field layer, the level of the taller flowering plants, like foxgloves and the fern uncurled. Next comes the shrub layer – bushes and young trees – and above that, quite an appreciable gap (depending on the nature of the woodland) before the penthouse suite, the canopy, the umbrella formed for the whole woodland by the crowns of mature trees.

That, then is the house. But a house is not a home, they say, without the cries of children – and the real children of the New Forest (Captain Marryat notwithstanding) are the birds. They are the creatures who give life and laughter, who turn an ornament into an organism. They are the twinkling jewels in the superb mounting.

It is possible that the Forest's first feathered tenants were nuthatch, tree-creeper, nightingale, woodcock and spotted woodpecker because they enjoy tree intensity – and 5,000 years ago the forests of Britain were more than twenty times their present size. These deep-wood birds were more abundant then, and so too, one suspects, was the hawfinch because its favourite haunt even today is the depths of oak and hornbeam woodland.

Not a great deal has been written on the patterns of bird settlement through the ages, but it is not such a breathtaking leap into the unknown to state that all the birds we know – with the exception of estuarine and marine birds – probably began in a treed habitat, close to their food source, which is the only criterion one need ever really apply.

After that, the tale was of adaptation related directly to changes in land use. When trees *en masse* gave way to copses, fields, gardens and hedgerows, birds like the robin, blackbird, song thrush, mistle thrush, altered their manners so effectively that they thrived in the new, open-plan environment.

And seed-eaters like chaffinch, greenfinch and yellowhammer must have glorified in the exoticising of their diets when it became possible for them to feed in stubble fields and stackyards and on the seeds of weeds which sprang into existence only when the canopy had been breached to admit sunlight.

More recently, in conifer plantations, the titmice moved on to the Southern comfort of hemlock and lodgepole pine, like trying bourbon after beer – and though crossbill and redpoll siskin share the same tastes, they seem to satisfy them at different levels.

All these species are commonplace in the New Forest; and because the perambulation includes large areas where trees give way to grass and ooze, there is also the marshland format with its own inhabitants – lapwing, snipe, curlew, redshank and other shore birds which fly inland for their food and then back to the sea-edge for peace of mind at night.

Drier heathlands accommodate whitethroats, dunnocks, blackbirds, larks – and the Dartford warbler, the shy little VIP most usually associated with the moors of the New Forest and the Wessex heathland.

Fears are often expressed for the safety and continuation of the breed when dry spells of weather are marked out geographically by areas of blackened earth. But to my mind, the Dartford may well have something of the phoenix about it. I can well believe it makes its escape ahead of the smoke and that the real consideration is not so much for a bird obliterated by a man-made phenomenon (very few blazes are 'acts of God') but for a fellow fussy about his privacy who keeps clear when there may be an accommodation problem.

Pam Harvey Richards puts the prospect in a nutshell when she says: 'If the Dartford warbler has any sense – and to hear the conservationists, you would think he is positively supernatural – then he moves out ahead of the fire and finds another bush. There are plenty of them' – this last a little wryly, because Pam can remember the time when you could ride from Red Shoot to Stoney Cross without veering your path for furze – and that's a Commoner kind of argument.

The thing about having a massive woodland to hand is that your garden on the periphery plays host to far more unusual guests than sparrow, starling, blackbird, thrush and the usual suburban round. In recent weeks, a green woodpecker has paced our lawn – looking decidedly uneasy, it's true, while gulls swooped and mouthed sailor curses overhead; taking himself to task, no doubt, that he ever dropped the habit of tree trunk totality to seek softer resistance and more seasonal fare. Goldfinches – these most highly coloured of U.K. inhabitants which so enchanted Richard Jefferies when he thought and wrote in his orchard at Coate – are frequent visitors; while great tits, bluetits, coal and long-tail live out their tiered existence in microcosm between Sitka spruce and Lawson cypress.

And on the chimney, content and cooing atop an almost natural echo chamber, perches the collared dove with a song that is no more and no less than an orchestration of indrawn breath. Never had I thought of birdsong as being a part of respiration until I sat before the unmade fire and listened to a draught being turned into a melody.

When I collected my thoughts about the proper form for this bird section, I thought, for a change (or at least, for a rather less familiar approach), I would deal with them by their songs. I would make the point that you might well be in the presence of a real avian curiosity which, hidden by foliage, would be lost to you – unless you could identify it by listening.

In my book, you can keep your birds of paradise, your parakeets, mynahs and budgerigars, your Technicolor wanderers. The jungle dwellers may flash upon the outward eye but they are doomed when they open their beaks, doomed to discord. I love the British birds, humble of plumage, noble of throat. And of all the birds, I love best the one whose name I knew first.

David Lack's observation is that the robin is a natural aggressor, that he spends a significant part of his life in battle. While I see sparrow dust-ups daily and blackbird confrontations that are all sound and fury, signifying nothing, I have yet to see my robins strike a blow in anger or out of it.

I have two – Robin North and Robin South – each of whom has introduced me to his family – and they confirm another impression I gained at that Bolderwood sketching session. If you will pardon the liberty, this is what I wrote:

> Red George beats his boundaries on the last day of October
> – That is the function of Samhain,
> For making territories plain –
> In fact, he beats them every day until his life is over.
> He cannot fence around a zone,
> So he must *say* what is his own.

His intermittent rattle song falls first upon the morning.
His nights are troubled and unsure,
In truth, he never feels secure.
He beats the blackbird to the post to issue a stern warning:
'Let no bird poach on my preserve,
I may be small but I have nerve.'

Thus he begins his repertoire, but lest it make him weary
– Too long a sermon of rebuke
Can be as tuneless as a rook –
He has two other songs in store, one sorrowful, one cheery,
A sigh for the contentious earth,
A bubbling of contented mirth.

No time of day, no depth of light will govern his expression.
He sings three songs within the hour.
What makes him sweet? What turns him sour?
To human power of reasoning, he will make no concession
– Does melody hide his sadness?
Does he winnow out of gladness?

If Red George keeps his mysteries as he protects his living,
No need to treat the world with scorn,
Nor lay the law down with each dawn.
Then he can slumber peacefully and banish all misgiving,
For trespassers are quite undone
With three songs for the price of one.

And that, I suppose, showed the weakness of my identifying-by-birdsong plan. For you cannot tie one bird to one song except in the most general terms and birds are not so much creatures of idiom as creatures of idiosyncrasy. While species may share a common timbre, each individual carries on his or her own conversation.

What are you to make, for instance, of just two of the blackbirds who split the pickings in our garden? One has never sung the same phrase twice and prefers not to be seen when he utters. The other, who fathered two broods this year, had plenty to say but mostly said this: 'I've got a daughter, yes, I have – dee-diddle-dee-da-da.' The diction was unmistakable, the meaning clear because frequently his chubby, brown, stubby-tailed offspring was sampling our insect life.

You may think the fact gave birth to the fancy – that no bird will ever deliver such sentences. Well, I have never heard such a persistent motif and I prefer to consider it a close encounter of the most positive kind. Much closer, certainly, than my first meeting with a great spotted woodpecker, at the top end of Bolderwood near the deer sanctuary. Strolling at 6.30 a.m., I think I caught him unawares because, although he gave no word of complaint, he made the most conscientious efforts to keep the width of his conifer meal-table between us.

Skylarks, thrusting towards Heaven, may be said to possess the highest common factor – but the similarity is in the 'unpremeditated' state of their 'profuse strains', as Percy Bysshe Shelley, no stranger to the Forest, was at pains to point out. For all that, a lark heard at any point takes me straight back to the same place – a cemetery on a hill above Bedwas in the Lower Rhymney Valley of South Wales where two people I learned to love and respect now lie buried. In fair weather, the larksong comes down there in showers; in drizzle, the undeterred song is a fall of sunbeams.

At certain times and at certain altitudes, there isn't too much difference between a titmouse and a butterfly. Butterflies don't sing, of course. But in a plantation where the bell-like tone of the great tit and the twitter of his blue cousin, the 'dit-dit' of the robin and the 'oh-dear' of the wren are the background to any and all scenes, the mouse method of moving in gangs is far more of a pointer to type than any attempt to pull one thread from the musical tapestry.

So I drop the names and I show the pictures and I reveal one heartening experience which has, happily, been my own.

I was a city boy, knew a sparrow when I saw one but never dreamt there might be a difference between hedge and house. My first recollection of a seagull was as a grey statue upon a grey rock, with grey water charging a weir under a grey sky in some unremembered place. For the rest, my knowledge was of the inanimate kind, picked up in museums with the sincere belief that those stuffed and spread-winged objects had never had an existence outside that glass case. I grew up learning that this was slightly less than the truth. But it is not until recent years that I have begun to appreciate that the birds have lives – nay, *personalities* – of their own. This rural renaissance of mine has been conducted entirely in the New Forest – by accident of circumstance, perhaps, but I am none the less grateful for that.

It happens that, in an antique shop in Lyndhurst, no longer there, I discovered three collections of Richard Jefferies essays, edited by Samuel J. Looker, which won me to the side of nature by the beauty of their words and the Agnes Miller Parker illustrations.

It happens that, on holidays which became ever more frequent, my family and I had 'time to stand and stare' to let this new awareness take hold.

It happens that I am now able to earn a living here in the Forest area and still have time to make the miracle grow.

My advantages are eyes to see, other senses to stimulate, a notebook to put all these things together – qualifications within the reach of most people.

So I drop names, I give you a push and I say, 'Go.'

Go wanting to learn what trees and creatures can tell you – and it is surprising how your knowledge will swell. I sincerely believe that Forest life can pick out the bona fide searchers as one used to be able to pick out Christians. In the same Messianic act of charity, the good news is made available to the genuine.

The American grey squirrel was introduced to Britain late last century. But as far as the New Forest is concerned, it came without an invitation, arriving in January, 1940, almost undoubtedly from the direction of Bournemouth. The Sandy City – as roving puppeteer Walter Wilkinson called it, not without venom – has had a colony of bannertails for many years, and it is as well we start our study there because at the beginning may well be found the right true end for the grey fellow.

The difference between the Bournemouth grey squirrel and the Forest grey squirrel is one of attitude – not only attitude by but attitude towards. In the seafront gardens, he is a charmer, a favourite; in the inland plantations, he is a tree-rat, a menace.

The first black mark against him is that he allegedly put the native red squirrel – a much prettier rodent – to flight. And that is a fallacy. The red, as Brian Vesey-Fitzgerald points out from a lifetime of experience, is quite capable of going into a decline without any help from an 'aggressor'. He noted a peak in Forest reds in 1908 and a dramatic falling away in 1909; such a build-up in the 1920s that control measures were necessary and another drop in 1929; a recovery by the late 1930s and a gradual degeneration (or redistribution) over the next 20 years, which just happened to coincide with the firm establishment of the grey.

Some say the grey and the red fought. Not so. In the one remaining pocket of co-habitation, around the Beaulieu parkland, they are happy side by side. More likely, they *competed* for limited spoils and Beatrix Potter's Nutkin found it a better strategy to seek pastures new. Certainly, that is the pattern in the mountainous woodlands of Wales, where the reds take the high ground and the greys are quite content with the valley bottoms. In nuisance terms, the woodman could find nothing to choose between them – they both enjoy a diet of seeds, acorns, insects, birds' eggs and – when pushed – fledglings.

And the controls exercised for the red fifty years ago in the Forest are

Grey squirrel – cursed by Foresters, cossetted by the public.

largely the same as those used against the grey today – even down to some of the trapping devices . . . although, thankfully, the 'squoils', heavy sticks discharged by the peasantry as a sport at an earlier date, have now fallen out of use or become for ever lodged in high branches.

In Bournemouth, helpful habits have been formed and the lesson is clear: give a squirrel a nut and he will leave your seeds alone; appease his hunger and he will leave the bark on your saplings. Bournemouth Parks Department, who are quite as conscientious about their young conifers as the Forestry Commission, find very few instances of the stripping which incenses the Forester up the road – they'd swop his squirrels for their vandals, any day.

Food is the bannertail's first priority. He is not fussy, but he must have it. In the Pleasure Gardens, the options are plentiful and the pickings so unhazardous that he will come and take a peanut from your fingers . . . and then bury it and forget where he put it, but that is by the way.

St Peter's Churchyard, one road back from the parkside, has fewer visitors and the behaviour of its squirrel congregation is that much more reserved. A degree of suspicion intrudes. But when they are in the presence of a donor, the word gets around. On a sunny day, from a seat among the resting-places of the Beales and the Tregonwells, I have offered them sandwiches, cold meat, potato crisps and seen them come within six inches of taking the fare – and then halt, quivering, waiting for me to let go so they can grasp and bounce away.

At Horseshoe Common, moving northward away from the town centre, the reluctance is even more marked. There, they will scatter at the rustle of a paper bag, and oft-times they will put the good solid width of a tree-trunk between them and you and rotate around it in direct counter to your own advance. And yet, cross the park early enough and you will see them fingering their way down the wire-netting of the litter-baskets to see what the humans have thrown away.

Walking to work through Horseshoe Common taught me two things about grey squirrels; first, that they do not hibernate – I have seen them as busy in December and January as at any high summer; second, that the degree of caution seems to relate directly to the degree of advance. Also, a bit of nonsense:

'Squirrels don't like the rain.
When they hear it on the window-pane,
They stay inside
Beside
Their nutshell fires . . .

Even within the Forest itself, there are variables. Nowhere does the bannertail become as blasé as his coastal brothers, but at places like the Brock Hill car park, at the head of the Rhinefield Ornamental Walks, he is a little less wary about letting himself be seen – and certainly, his food horizons are being widened to encompass tripper debris.

All of which would seem to indicate that he can be taught modes rather less destructive than those he now practises, probably in all innocence. That being so, perhaps the more fruitful policy would be to encourage him rather than to meet him with snare-boxes and small-bore shotguns, which will only move him deeper into the woodland and farther away from the possibility of adapting to less controversial sustenance.

The Forestry Commission contention, of course, is that it is hard enough now to keep the grey within controllable figures, but the argument is based solely on the equation of squirrel versus tree. And until there emerges a sizeable desire to win the grey over to haute cuisine, their suspicions are understandable. The experiment would be no good, after all, if the alternative food was not forthcoming. It would be at just such a time that the hungry rodent would start tearing the place apart and proving that his opponents were right all along.

But the potshot thinking, I say, is all wrong – and the 5p-a-tail bounty introduced in certain areas when infestation gets out of hand, in the Commission's understanding, is downright dangerous. Sooner flying fur than flying lead. Certainly, a lot less can go wrong . . .

Besides, all of this leaves aside a factor whose influence is of epidemic proportions and whose blood-red manifestation along any stretch of Forest road renders the best figures available inaccurate in a very short space of time. It is the 'squoil' of today, the petrol-driven guided missile directed upon any item of wildlife foolish enough to cross its path in defiance (or ignorance) of its punishing speed.

And even if nothing more comes of this whimsical plan of mine to have the woodman's greatest enemy feeding from his hand, I would at least make him one exhortation: count the number of crushed corpses which litter the tarmac before you decide how many more are going to have to die.

That is a plea which might well be repeated for the benefit of the Forest's largest set of mammals – the deer. And for similar reasons, since the uncaring driver does not seem to be deterred by the size of his prey.

But for the deer, I would never suggest the cultivation of domesticity. If roe and fallow, red and Sika ever became as commonplace as cows, they would lose me. I can stand on the observation platform at Bolderwood now and see them lazing and grazing on the protected meadows towards Bratley Wood, and know . . . that this isn't the animal I want to see, nor the way I like to see it. I might as well be visiting a zoo.

A great part of the Forest's appeal where it is thickest, deepest, quietest is that there is always the chance but never the certainty of seeing deer. You tread carefully, negotiating a thin line between the carelessness that cracks twigs and the sinister step that hints at menace. And when contact comes, there is an exhilaration in the explosion of surprise – a small neat head rising from a sea of ferns to regard you with something close to derision (no animal is better at looking down its nose); the white flash of a roe rump and birch leaves shimmering in the draught of its turn.

The experts tell you that the best time to see deer is just before sunset, when they quit their cover and come forth to feed in the rides and on the lawns, but that is not hard and fast.

The noblest stag I have seen – an eight-to-ten pointer – was a bonus in the mid-day sun when I stopped the car on the Lyndhurst-Christchurch road, with Markway Inclosure on my left and open plain leading to young plantings and then on to Shoot Wood to my right. A court of hinds could be seen grazing near young Scots pines, and then, just as I was thinking I would leave them to their meal, the sire swung into view, his antlers so heavy that his head was bowed.

His harem were obviously of his genre. The form of his branches labelled him unmistakably red – one of the originals, those the Conqueror was said to love 'like a father'. I was being privileged to view some of the mere 30 or so reds now left in the Forest.

It is probable that the reds were an endangered species by the time the mediaeval monarchs withdrew their attention from the Forest as a hunting ground. Even before the zeal which followed the Deer Removal Act (1851) there were not more than 80 known to be in the woodlands and today, by reason of their scarcity, they are exempted from the seasonal culls.

Their haunts are widely distributed, tending more towards the south-east of the Forest – Hawkhill, Stubbs Wood, Tantany Wood area. Until the early 1960s, a few were known to operate north of the Ringwood-Cadnam road and a few more between that road and the Southampton-Bournemouth railway line.

Because both stags and hinds are known to exist, it is not immediately clear why they remain so sparse, but it may be that the red, with the deepest roots of the local deer, have found it harder to adapt to the increased coming and going through Forest demesnes. It is a biological fact that they put more store on privacy for their affairs than any of the more recent 'imports'.

The red is the largest of the Forest deer. Mature stags stand some 100–120 cm. (40–48 in.) high at the shoulder and weigh approximately 122 kg. (270 lb.). Hinds stand about 95 cm. (37 in.) tall and weigh up to 73 kg. (160 lb.).

They take on their rich, dark-red summer coat in May and change it for dark-brown with varying amounts of grey in winter, when the stag develops a mane. Calves are born, in June, with spots which they lose in five or six weeks for a dull brown fluffy coat.

These days, claims one Forest-loving friend of mine, you cannot sit down for a picnic without running the risk of being trampled by fallow deer. Well, such has never been my happy experience but the fallow, without a doubt, comes closest to being plentiful.

The males are bucks, the females does and the young, fawns. There is a tradition – which doesn't, actually, go back any further than 100 years when the cult of the expert began to emerge – that the fallow were introduced to the Forest by Romans/Phoenicians/Gauls, but the more plausible theory is that they came with the Normans.

In the last 900 years, their fortunes have undulated. A census taken in 1670 put the fallow population at seven-and-a-half thousand, almost certainly an under-estimate with the optimum figure nearer 8,000. From then on, the numbers declined, not (only) because of hunting but because output began to exceed food supply. An 1830 census put the figure at just over 5,000 and one taken at the time of the Deer Removal Act, 4,000.

Though the enthusiasts bade fair to rid the Forest of deer at Queen Victoria's behest, they failed to such a degree that by 1877 the beasts were back to making a nuisance. That prompted the annual cull which still takes place, though to a lesser extent. Deputy Surveyor Gerald Lascelles estimated in 1892 that there were a mere 250 fallow in attendance. The present figure, largely maintained, is about 800–900 spread over most of the Forest except in the south and south-east where, possibly, the competition from the red is too stiff.

The fallow are not averse, however, to advancing within sight of their larger cousins – and one of the best places for deer-spotting is north of the stretch of railway line between Brockenhurst and Beaulieu Road in the rides and lawns that punctuate Pignal Wood, Perry Wood and Woodfidley. I always enjoy a train breakfast – and like it all the more for the sight of small fallow family groups with the same intention.

The fallow, for some genetic reason tied in with their profusion, occasionally produce a white buck, whose manifestation upon an inn sign is seen in most Forest villages. But only Ringwood's Market Square has the Original White Hart where, it is said, a hunting party containing Henry VIII, Archduke Philip of Spain and his wife, Joan, and lords and ladies, had taken refreshment after running a celebrated local buck, Albert, to a standstill in a nearby meadow. On a plea from the ladies, Albert was not killed. On the same day, Sir Halliday Wagstaffe, Keeper of Woods and

Fallow deer crossing open land near the Bolderwood deer sanctuary – most widespread of the Forest deer.

narrator of the account, was knighted. Henry was obviously in one of his more expansive moods. The full story is told on a plaque fixed to the outside wall near the inn entrance.

The white buck – strictly speaking, he is off-white, veering towards cream – has been given a mystical persona over the years, first in the ancient Celtic verse of Amergin and lately in the novel of the same name by artist Sven Berlin, whom we shall be meeting before very long. The work, as well as giving the Forest its first hint of something more super than natural, happens to reveal more of Berlin's own feelings about the Forest than even his autobiographical piece, *Dromengro*. And for him, strangely, the fantasy came some 20 years after the fact – his sculpture of the white buck was commissioned for – of all places – a synthetic rubber factory at Fawley in 1958, as a reminder that, in the most unlikely places, art will flourish with all the zest of poppies on roadworks and that at least one industrialist was not hog-tied to the balance sheet.

Roe deer, although only half as plentiful as fallow in the Forest (they average 400–500, but estimates are probably on the low side) still have a rather exceptional status – vermin rather than venison – which means they can be taken at any time.

The summer coat is a bright reddish-brown. The ears are large and black-bordered framing a short, blunt face. The caudal disc at rear – and that is, on balance, the most likely way you will see them, bounding away – lacks the black surrounds of the fallow and sika. In does, the disc is heart-shaped; in bucks, kidney-shaped. Winter colouring is grey or grey-brown. The young roe – kids or fawns – are born in May and their pelage is light-brown, flecked with white, but this soon changes to a dull uniform brown which only gains its richness with maturity. By October, the youngsters have gained the adults' winter colouring.

The ready availability of roebuck keeps the wheels turning for John Frederick Strange, of Lyndhurst, latest in a line of butchers whose New Forest connections go back more than 200 years.

Normal culling season is August-February and although Mr Strange has all the latest deep-freeze refinements not to have to worry too greatly about time, he prefers to serve his venison customers (and, indeed, all the others) with fresh meat. His sausages go all over the world and in particular to an airfield in Basra. Foreign tourists load their freezer boxes and the buyer down from London just for the purpose is not uncommon. In fact, Forest supplies are not sufficient and the Strange larder is swelled from the Berkley Estate in Gloucestershire and from Woburn.

For all that, Mr Strange has no truck with back-door suppliers whose sources are questionable, and damaged meat – accident victims – goes to kennels but never to the Strange shelves.

Although he works according to tradition, it is his wife, Desirée – a 'foreigner' from the West Country – who is the historian, and with the Chamber of Trade she has recently produced a pamphlet on Lyndhurst past and present.

Venison as meat? 'It is always lean,' says Mr Strange, 'and doctors recommend it.'

How so? 'No force feeding, no antibiotics. The deer live on the herbs and the organic greenery, and as a result the meat is clean – no danger of anything nasty getting into the food-chain.'

Roe are thought to have become extinct in Southern England some time between the 14th and 17th centuries and the present Forest herd are likely to have re-colonised the area from 1890 onward, having spent the rest of that century spreading across Dorset from Milton Abbas. Now, they can be found all over the Forest but concentrate in the Holmsley/Wilverly area and are seldom seen south-east of the Beaulieu River.

The other two species are innovations, pure and simple.

The Japanese sika deer, found to the south of the main Southampton-Bournemouth railway line in the vicinity of New Copse, Hawkhill and Stockley Inclosures, are all descendants of four animals released from the Beaulieu estate in 1904–5. Their summer coat is bright chestnut with yellow spots; winter takes away the spots and grants them a darker, longer coat. They affect the branch-like antlers of the red deer, on a correspondingly smaller scale.

The Chinese muntjac were liberated in Britain from Woburn Park about 1900, and with further escapes from private collections they have formed quite a sizeable presence in suitable areas of Central and Southern England. They run to only short antlers but do have extended canine teeth protruding from the upper jaw. They are pig-like in stature – which makes them probably the closest creature the British woodlands now boast to the long-departed wild boar. In the New Forest, they have been recorded at Parkgrounds Inclosure, Matley Wood and Mark Ash, which would seem to indicate a spread not entirely reflected by the isolation of the sightings. Elsewhere, I note my own suspicions that they could well be fairly numerous among the ferns of Broomy and Spring Bushes.

Muntjac do not figure significantly in any culling figures for the reasons already outlined. They keep, as we say these days, a low profile.

Red deer, for reasons of antiquity, are administered more for humane motives than with any thought of control. Roebuck, as stated, are game any time of the year – but that still means you break the law if you relax them without a licence or at night or with the wrong calibre of weapon.

As far as any criteria exist, the extent and system of culling still follow the recommendations of Arthur Cadman. Allowing for an annual growth rate of 33 per cent in any particular species, he theorised, your culling ratio was going to have to be 34 per cent or more.

At the younger end of the scale, extinction would be limited to 'poor beasts', the justification being their long-term effect on the standard of the herd – an equal number of male and female animals.

Males, of course, are distinguishable in the field by their antler development and the Cadman system envisages two (out of a hundred) of the 2–3- and 3–4-year-olds, and one each of the rest up to eight years of age. No kills of beasts between eight and ten and two of beasts over ten, but for humaneness rather than control. Females, far harder to date in the field during their middle years, would be culled to the extent of five in every hundred, with four in every hundred taken because they had become old and feeble.

Today, the criteria are largely unchanged – with one major difference. When Donn Small took over as Deputy Surveyor, he found that the business of culling was in the hands of 'sportsmen', many from Continental countries and even more who put enthusiasm above accuracy. 'My staff found deer coping with terrible gunshot wounds or dying slowly because somebody's aim had been off,' he told me. 'I thought if we had to kill them at all, let us, at least, make a decent job of it.'

Now only Forestry Commission marksmen or shots of proven ability are allowed officially within range of the deer. I say 'officially' because there remains a measure of poaching, particularly on the Brockenhurst side of the Forest.

Thankfully, the long dogs and the cutting wire have gone from this area – though they persist on the neighbouring Cranborne Chase (but that is another book), much to the chagrin of the Nature Conservancy and Royal Society for the Prevention of Cruelty to Animals, who have to deal with the results.

The Forestry Commission's answer to my point about the haphazard 'control' provided by fast and fearless drivers is, of course, a simple one; the vehicular vandals seldom pause to check whether their victims fulfil the requirements I have outlined. In addition, not all accident victims die on the spot; many of them drag themselves or, at best, limp away and have to be cut down at a later date for reasons which would find agreement from even the most vehement of deer champions once he had seen how the creatures were suffering from their impact injuries.

Though I cannot – and probably will never – quite shake off the Bambi syndrome, I have to admit that I would sooner be a deer in the Forest today than one that took its chances just a few years ago. Given that I never went near any roads . . .

The rabbits of the Forest area display a Watership Down tenacity which develops quite often into a kind of foolhardiness for which they pay with the only currency they have available.

Myxomatosis, started as a good idea by a French doctor on his own entirely inadequate estate, reached the Forest in Spring 1954 via the English Channel (somehow), Sussex and Hampshire. The disease had its fling up until late 1955 and rabbit numbers since have not recovered sufficiently to present Foresters with a major problem. They are content to regard the situation as being contained by predators – owl, hobby, sparrowhawk.

The response of the rabbits – perhaps they have read Richard Adams, too – has been to boldly go where no rabbit has gone before.

I know of a research establishment adjoining (and encompassing) a former airfield where the lengthening spring evenings can be made merry for the watchers beyond the wire as the rabbit families graze and take their sport along the field's wooded edge. But it is no fun when you find humans

Donkeys. Coming into the Forest from the north, you may spot a donkey before a pony. Elsewhere, the ponies have the monopoly.

stiffening and sniffing the air at the crack of a rifle, and it is hardly practical to have your mood for the day ruined by finding that the Defence Ministry custodians have cut the grass.

The situation was obviously becoming a little frustrating for the animals themselves, because one evening, circling a smallish landscaped roundabout on a nearby Forest road, I was amazed to find four rabbits – two large, two small – feeding away at the scant lawn between the odd berberis, gorse and silver birch. It was, I thought, not much of a place to raise a family.

Adams, in his acknowledgement to R.M. Lockley as a source, speaks of his surprise at the sophistication of the rabbit society. (And he certainly makes it memorable in literary terms. If I had written one book in my life, I would have wished it to be that one.) And now here, not fifty crow miles from the downs of Watership – which lies between Whitchurch and Kingsclere, in North Hants – were this little family, completely walled in by the kingdom of the *hrududu*, chewing away nonchalantly so close to the passing cars that they could probably feel the draught.

The prospect chilled me. I took to varying my journeys so that I could keep the roundabout under observation and at first it looked as though my fears were going to be realised. There was one flattened ragbag of brown fur in the road and then, on the opposite side of the turn, there was another. Father? Mother? Children? Was this how all of them would stop running?

One's mind begins to work along impractical lines. What about a sign – 'Beware of rabbits'? It gave an entirely wrong emphasis, and 'Look out for rabbits' made it seem like an invitation to remove your attention from a fairly tricky driving manoeuvre. Or a fence around the island? Well, we knew what rabbits thought of fences. And all this would need planning permission, public inquiries, new byelaws? Surely, that would take too long and the rabbits would be gone, anyway. The problem seemed insoluble – because none of us would give the rabbits credit for providing their own answer.

But somehow, you don't see corpses these days – just the little live ones chewing the cud and looking not in the least concerned as the traffic ruffles their fur. I suppose now I should begin to wonder whether exhaust fumes might start to stunt their growth, but I'll wager they have an answer to that, too.

The rest of the Forest fauna are rather more predictable. The boar probably died out during the fifteenth century – though Charles II tried unsuccessfully to reintroduce it, probably with the idea of selling tickets for hunts. Its modern-day counterpart, the 'Hampshire hog', is to be found foraging along the roadsides at Bramshaw, Fritham and Minstead and – believe me – its present size allied with the tusks of its forebear would make it a quarry of rhinoceros proportions.

The wolf was extinct by the early 16th century; the marten lingered in South Hampshire until the 19th century; the hare, seemingly unaffected by the mid-20th century pestilence, is to be found in abundance on the moorlands and appears to thrive despite occasional tussles with the beagles.

The fox is listed as a useful controller of populations among smaller mammals and his diet has been extended to include wood-mice, voles, moles, rats and squirrels since rabbits went through their thin time.

It is difficult to put a number on the badgers in the Forest because their habits are so furtive, but a reasonable statement might be – 'More than you think.' Again, sadly, your only daylight sighting may be of the post-mortem variety as the demon driver strikes again; or of the indirect variety, where a large hole in the ground in a broadleaf inclosure may prove to be a sett and well-used runs will chart the badger's nocturnal journeyings.

There are otters in the Forest – at least, the otter hunters who until so recently made their annual visit to the Brockenhurst area seemed to think so – but I have never seen one and it is likely that Tarka's friends stick to the lower reaches of the Forest's waterways (hardly wide enough to be termed rivers).

The stoat and weasel tend to come and go in relation to the numbers of rabbits, mice and voles which form their prey. The dormice, having lost their favourite habitat of hazel coppice, in the interests of successful silviculture, have tended to move out on to the downs of Cranborne Chase, where a good hurdle-maker can still find a profit in a stand of hazel.

The rise and fall of long-tailed fieldmouse and yellow-necked fieldmouse coincide with gluts of beechmast, acorns, seeds or berries; otherwise, they are more often found in the better farming areas around Ringwood and the Avon Valley, Hordle/Everton and Milford/East End/Inchmery. Voles have occasional population booms which, apart from making their predators unduly fat, can sometimes affect the welfare of trees, where bark is gnawed away right down to the cambium layer.

To judge from the number of hedgehogs wiped out throughout the whole Forest and fringe area, their live total must be phenomenal – but since they feed on insects which might otherwise provoke a great deal of arboreal mayhem, they are welcomed.

Which is more than can be said for the mole in an area where fields are at a premium and where cricket pitches – Swan Green and Bolton's Bench, Lyndhurst; Burley; Godshill; Frogham, to name but a few – tend to be regarded with more than the usual seriousness. Besides, cricketers have troubles enough already – 'PSP' on the scorebook means 'pony stopped play', and that could be by wandering onto a green during the innings or visiting in between times and leaving more creases than are strictly necessary in the pitch.

There remain two sections of Forest life unrecorded and they are the kingdoms of wriggle and crawl – reptiles and insects.

I have to admit that snakes leave me cold. More than that, they make me cold – and because this was a piece of discrimination which no observer could allow in all conscience, I submitted myself to some shock therapy at the Holidays Hill reptiliary, off the A35 between Bolderwood and Swan Green. There, keeper Derek Taylor – a trained taxidermist before he joined the Forestry Commission – has created model environs for the Forest's cold blood . . . adder, grass snake and smooth snake, slow-worm (which is a lizard without legs, as you know, no doubt), sand lizard and heath lizard, common frog, Natterjack toad and common toad and three kinds of newt. These have been joined in a most congenial captivity by the black adder and the tree frog. In separate but adjacent apartments, all these creatures live out their destiny with the kiss of the sun for pardon and plenty of rocks on which to take its warmth; also, abundant cover when they need it – which would seem

Pony Stops Play . . . Straying animals are hazards peculiar to Forest cricket pitches like this one at Swan Green, Lyndhurst.

to be, on the date of my visit, most of the time.

I steeled myself for the ordeal and found, with a party of schoolboys and their master and their clipboards, that the name of the game was 'I spy'.

Spurred on by the need to stay cool, I made slow progress around the pits, switching my glance to follow every cry of 'There, it moved', 'See its eye', 'Under that rock' and the like. It would have been interesting to read the essays that resulted from that particular minibus foray, because imagination must have played a great part.

The newts were brash enough – they always are – but of lizards and frogs, there was no sign. The adder had found itself a corner and curled up like a catherine wheel.

When the boys had gone and I was beginning to lose my nerve, the black adder – he's the *really* dangerous one – crawled down a branch and drank so daintily from the pool in its compound that I began to understand why herpetologists can enthuse. The thing is certainly pretty, like a jewel necklace where the sun catches it. But one of my own? Well, not today, thank you.

Of the insects, the biting flies *(Tabanidae)* are the most troublesome and the dragon-flies (Southern Aeshna, demoiselle, damsel-fly) the most scintillating.

For colour alone, the Forest is said to boast nearly 2,000 species of butterfly and moth and enough could be said about them to make an excess of everything else here written.

The white admiral is on the wing in July at the edges of the oak woodlands where honeysuckle provides food for the larva. The silver-washed fritillary drifts and flutters across the rides and can be found feeding on bramble blossom in July and August. The brimstone makes two appearances in spring and August. The speckled wood spends the summer among deciduous woodland.

August and September bring forth the red admiral, peacocks, small tortoiseshells, commas and small coppers and throughout the summer, over the heathlands, flicker silver-studded blues, small heaths and graylings. Some years promote the green hairstreak and pearl-bordered fritillaries. The Glanville fritillary is also a possible sighting. But the purple emperor seems to have departed. A 1973 record lists the last Forest sighting as in 1947.

The moths, smaller and less resplendent, include the pine hawk, hummingbird hawk, elephant hawk, five-spot burnet, silver Y and common heath as well as a whole bundle of night-fliers which seem to enjoy roosting in the road ahead of car headlights – a not entirely sensible course of conduct.

On the subject of night-fliers – and on the argument of context rather than genus – we might here mention the bats. The Forest has eleven of the twelve recorded British species – Leisler's bat is the absentee – including the rare Bechstein's bat, the scarce Barbastelle, Noctule, Pipistrelle, Long-Eared, Natterer's and Whiskered.

Beetles include the Long-horn among the wood-borers, the stag and the Minotaur. Ponds and pools yield the medicinal leech, water spider, water boatman, water snail and whirligig. Other insects are plentiful and characteristic of the habitats available, acid soil, dry moorland, wet valley bottom, bog.

When the eye is dazzled, the fingers itch for possession and it might be timely now to direct the attention to the Forestry Commission Byelaws, 1971.

Section 5 (iv) forbids any person on the lands of the Forestry Commissioners to dig up, remove, cut or injure any tree, shrub or plant, whether living or not, or dig up or remove any soil, leafmould, moss, peat, sand, gravel or mineral of any kind – without a licence, that is: our tree gerontologist with his feet-long tube heading for the peat bogs would have made sure he had the necessary documentation.

Section 5 (ix) forbids the visitor to 'wilfully disturb, injure or destroy any bird, fish or animal.'

The barrack-room lawyer might argue that this still leaves certain (small) factors of wildlife for the taking but the spirit of the law is clear.

If it belongs to the Forest, leave it alone.

If you want to see it again, come back.

If it isn't there then, somebody else has broken the law – and broken laws are just a short step away from anarchy. You came here for peace, not anarchy.

Defence rests . . .

Church versus Rufus

THE Rufus Stone in Canterton Glen has today a nice dignity about it. The Forestry Commission has set up a corral-like access which, among the surrounding oaks and beeches of Canterton, gives the scene a wood-on-wood propriety.

True, there remains the iron casing (installed in 1841) which caused historian John Wise to remark (circa 1883): 'It stands . . . rather as a monument of the habit of that English public who imagine that their eyes are at their fingers' ends, and of a taste that is on a par with that of the designer of the post office pillar-boxes, than of the Red King's death . . .'

But there are worse things than pillar-boxes; and when writers of the 1920s and 1930s spoke of charabancs and coconut shies, you might imagine that there wasn't too much farther downward the site could go without hitting what the economists call an upsurge.

Well, perhaps the Forestry Commission thought so, too, because the nearest thing to a coconut shy visible on our day was a Bounty wrapper dropped in the car park. And charabancs seem to have given way largely to the ubiquitous caravanette and the occasional student-laden minibus.

Nobody expected the broadleaves, in their way, to throw up a cathedral to honour the spot where the bane of the clergy was felled. But at least the raucousness has been removed and what remains – quiet, thoughtful, giving out on to a broad and inspirational expanse – seems to confirm that this was a capital Event and not one of your lower-case variety.

Much has been written about the death of William Rufus but little can be trusted. The actual facts are so few that they might be said to provide the hole in the middle of the embroidery.

The two chroniclers closest to the final act were William of Malmesbury *(Gesta Regum Anglorum)* and Orderic Vitalis *(Historia Ecclesiastica)*. Much of their account is retrospective and prone to the special influences I shall outline later, but here, in the early evening of August 2, 1100, they placed the King and Walter Tirel (alone according to Malmesbury; with others, according to Vitalis) at the scene of the killing.

The sun was setting over Long Beech, no doubt in the same way as it has been setting for centuries before and since, scarlet in aspect and heavy on glare. A stag bounded out of the woods. The King shot and slightly wounded it. On it went up the hill towards the lowering orb. The King stood watching it, shading his eyes with his hands. At that moment, another beast of chase broke cover and Tirel shot at it. His arrow skimmed the beast's back. An arrow lodged in Rufus's chest. The King fell without a word, trying to pull out the shaft, which snapped in his hand.

With a remarkable lack of sorrow or ceremonial, the other named members of Rufus's hunting party took off in various directions – Walter Tirel to Poole and thence to Normandy; Rufus's brother, Henry, to Winchester and thence to the throne; William de Breteuil, keeper of the Treasury, chewing on Henry's dust all the way to Winchester to make a vain claim for power on behalf of the Conqueror's eldest son, Robert, to whom Rufus and Henry had sworn fealty and who was currently making a leisurely return to Britain from the Crusade; the others to their respective homes where, presumably, they would keep out of the way until matters should be resolved.

There is, or rather, was a belief among Forest gypsies that Rufus was killed 'not where that little bitti stone is . . . (but) up on Fritham Plain' – that statement delivered by one Benny Wells, of fairly modern times when somebody suggested he was old enough to remember the original incident – 'and as true as I'm standing here (may the Lord strike me if I lie) there's a pool not far off – where he bled, see – what runs red the self-same day he died.' The pond, according to William of Malmesbury, was at Finchhampstead, Berkshire, and the significance is not clear because it is nowhere near any route Rufus, dead or alive, might have taken. Local telling makes it Ocknell Pond, and on our own visit it reflected not mayhem but passing clouds. The scientific explanation is more likely to be a timely

The Rufus Stone. Described by John Wise as 'Of a taste on a par with that of the designer of the post office pillar-boxes'.

appearance of an alga like Palonella cruenta or Haematococcus sanguineus.

(The gypsies have a passionate love for the more lurid of details as well as a firm territorial sense, but before we give too much weight to their version it should be pointed out that the Forest's Romany influx came far closer to our time than the Rufus period.)

Duncan Grinnell-Milne, after a masterly appraisal of facts and nuances (*The Killing of William Rufus*, David and Charles, 1968), set out in the best classic tradition of the 'whodunnit', concludes that nothing can be found other than oral tradition, which is 'quicksand to the historian'. What makes the tradition rather more solid in this instance, he says, is that it carries 'the strength of simplicity'.

In fact, the very ground speaks for Canterton Glen.

Geoffrey Gaimar, around 1135, says that the King and Tirel were hunting 'in a densely wooded part of the Forest, near a marsh.' C.J. Cornish, around 1894, records that the land west of the Rufus Stone is a 'marshy slope' and adds: 'Wood does not grow on it now and never could have grown for the nature of the soil has not changed, and remains in the same condition . . . as in the days of the Conquest.'

Modern ecologists would confirm the principle. For my late 1970s evidence, I look to my wellington boots, marked well above the ankle with the depth of the soil treachery after only a moderate amount of rainfall. And the woods to either side are dense for a certainty, 'ancient and ornamental' in their repertoire of twisted oaks and thickened at head level with gorse, sloe and unfruitful crab apple.

Modern historian Arthur Lloyd makes a case for a site near the present Park Farm, on the Beaulieu Estate, quoting a section of the Annals of Waverley Abbey which speaks of a Cistercian Abbey named Bellus Locus 'near the spot where William Rufus the King was killed.' He strengthens his argument with Leland's 16th century reference to 'Thoroughham' as the point where death took place. Park Farm, he says, was once called Througham and there was known to have been a royal hunting lodge in the area. But the Rev. William Gilpin, of Boldre, suggested as long ago as 1790 that 'Thoroughham' might well have been Fritham. And if the derivation of names has any weight at all, there is a 'Park Farm' at Minstead, near Malwood.

Such contentions are hardly likely to be resolved beyond an agreement to disagree, and I would say only this – if the 'marshy conditions' mentioned prevail at Park Farm, Beaulieu Estate, it is surprising that the holding has provided a living for so long.

'Malwood' comes into the picture in T.W. Shore's *History of Hampshire*, where he says, purely in passing during a fairly short and entirely uncontroversial account of the assassination, that the King fell 'at Malwood'.

Malwood has been cut in two since antiquity by the Cadnam-Ringwood route, evolving from cart-track to dirt road, to A31 and, most recently, to M27. The 1973 Ordnance Survey Sheet SU 21/31 is explicit of this fragmentation but we can be even more so.

Malwood Farm still nestles safely on the Rufus Stone side of the Great Divide, with its adjoining woodland running straight and true up to Canterton Glen. On the southern side of the motorway, the name continues, with a smaller division – the delightful, shaded roadway that joins Minstead (Mintestede at Domesday) to the main thoroughfare – and it was from this point that the history of Malwood began.

To your left as you top the hill from Minstead is the old site of Malwood Lodge, where the warden of that section of the Forest had a residence – although arguably not as long ago as 1100. (In any event, you are unlikely to be able to form your own opinion because the area is now in the occupation of the Southern Electricity Board and the fences are high.) To your right are two most curious installations – one, a red-brick mansion running to seed and the other a roughly circular enclosure walled in earth, though at no point to any height.

The mansion was designed by Mr Evan Christian and built for the family of Sir William Harcourt, who, in 1894 as Chancellor of the Exchequer, introduced death duties – not a great deal for which to be remembered. Today the house, which has a slight gingerbread gothic air about it, has been converted into flats and women converse across courtyards window to window, children play under washing lines and men tinker with their cars. The nearby earthworks, named on the map as Malwood Castle, a fort, are overgrown and hard to find.

'Malwood' is not mentioned by the earliest chroniclers of the killing and those who have remarked it since do it without a great deal of on-the-ground conviction.

The lodge where Rufus was said to have eaten his last meal could, in fact, be on either side of the Minstead-motorway road. But it seems to me that some kind of lightly fortified motte and bailey construction like this would be far more likely to provide accommodation for a king and his hunting party – which could number at least 100 persons counting guests, retainers and court-followers – than the place across the way, which would probably house only the warden, his family and a minimal staff.

But I said the story began here. 'Malwood' – despite some adroit juggling with the Old French 'malvoute' and 'malvoisin', words Rufus was known to have used to describe Westminster Hall, which Ranulf Flambard had designed for him, and a tower erected to threaten Bamburgh during the 1095 revolt – undoubtedly had a far simpler genesis. For here one Malf was known to have held 3½ hides of land from Edward the Confessor. By 1087, the Domesday Book had this to say: 'Here, the sons of Malf held land of the King . . . Now, in the time of William, it is ½ a hide; the rest is in the Forest.'

That is a simple statement of accounting which could have indicated a certain measure of respect for the resident family from the afforesting Conqueror whereby he took the trees but retained the name; a cause of grievance which might one day erupt into violence of the most lethal kind;

even – in the propagandising years after the assassination – just a particularly evil mediaeval pun!

So much for the scene of the crime – for crime it certainly was, conceived in advance, even advertised in advance, with righteousness rather than malice aforethought. That much emerges unquestionably from what I earlier called the embroidery – the lacework of dreams, portents and sermonic promises to and by nobles and churchmen who were privy (if not party) to the killing.

But before we begin to study motives, let us spare a moment for means.

All accounts favour bow and arrow, though because Orderic Vitalis once refers to 'catapulta' rather than 'sagitta' (which he mentions on at least six other occasions) a belief that the killing impact came from a cross-bow or arbalest bolt rather than the conventional arrow has proved convenient for at least one theory.

Certainly, the Anglo-Saxon Chronicler understood the difference. Of a man shot in Normandy in the Conqueror's time, he writes: He was killed by a bolt from a cross-bow; of Rufus's slaying, he writes that the King 'was killed by an arrow.' The Malmesbury writings make the same distinction throughout. Furthermore, it is this account which states: 'Clutching at the shaft where it protruded from his breast, the King fell forward, breaking the arrow as he hit the ground' – a strange thing for a steel bolt to do.

Earlier, as he had been dressing for the hunt, he had been approached by the fletcher (possibly Cobb of Eling, who supplied missiles when the Conqueror and his family were in the Forest, from 1079) and given six brand-new arrows, two of which Rufus passed to Tirel with the words, 'The best arrows for the best shot.'

The suggestion seems to be that it was one of these shafts which caused death, although nobody actually makes that point.

There are fairly logical arguments against. If Tirel were the assassin, would he be likely to use one of those two telltale arrows? After all, two arrows would hardly be a sufficient quiverload for a hunt. Again, if Tirel were not the killer, what an essential part of the frame it would be to ensure that an arrow so marked should be the one that penetrated the royal bosom – there being, of course, more than six such arrows in circulation.

It remains no stronger than an inference, bearing more on intention than on actual execution, and the matter unresolved serves to give strength (or perhaps currency is a better word) to the supernatural interpolations of Hugh Ross Williamson, who seems to find a certain amount of heavy breathing among Rufus's courtiers, Mithras worshippers as they all apparently were.

To understand why a man should die, it helps to understand how he lived.

Shadows lengthen through the autumn woodland near the scene of William Rufus's death.

William of Malmesbury describes Rufus's appearance thus: 'He was small and thick set and ill-shaped, yet having enormous strength. His face was redder than his hair and his eyes were of two different colours. His vices were branded on his face.' A court portrait painter, at the turn of the 12th century, it seems, would have needed to be something of a Picasso.

A profile from a coin of the era in fact shows common lines to those of the face of Vlad Tepes (Vlad Dracul, Vlad the Impaler), the mid-European monarch of the 13th century who inspired the Dracula legend before Bram Stoker got hold of it, on the grounds of displaying appetites similar to those attributed to Rufus – not that that gives us a vampire in the Forest, however much Margaret Murray and Hugh Ross Williamson might welcome it.

Adds William of Malmesbury: 'He was brave; he honoured his father's memory; he could at times act wisely and with decision.' Orderic Vitalis says: 'He was imperious, daring and war-like and gloried in the pomp of his numerous troops. His memory was very tenacious and his efforts to keep the peace throughout his dominions were unceasing.'

In the mid-19th century, E.A. Freeman *(Reign of William Rufus)* finds fuel for condemnation in the colour of the King's countenance. Red was the colour of the blood he spilled, of the deer he hunted, of the Devil himself and the flames of Hell, to which Freeman consigned Rufus before his pen ran dry. No wife, no mistress, no string of hedge-begots meant to Freeman that the man was a sodomist and a homosexual.

A little later, John R. Wise added that Rufus, without any of the Conqueror's ability or power of statesmanship, 'inherited all his vices, which he so improved that they became rather his own.'

Freeman's come-uppance came in J.H. Round's essays in historical detection *(Feudal England)*. 'We see that in all these fantasies,' wrote Round after an examination of pathological intensity on Freeman's wildest claims, 'we have what can only be termed history in masquerade.' Freeman first formed the theory, said Round, and then, under its spell, fitted the facts to it without question.

Frank Barlow *(The Feudal Kingdom of England, 1042–1216)* did as much as any to answer Wise's claims and readjust the balance generally. While conceding shortcomings – Rufus had 'little personal dignity . . . a simulated bluster and a threatening countenance' – he credited Rufus with never behaving unnaturally towards his kin, cherishing the memory of his parents and crushing his enemies with less chicanery than his father had used and certainly less savagery. 'The Norman Church was to welcome his strong rule and to think his mocking jests a small price to pay for peace and order,' he said.

But propagandising for Church and/or State is not the prerogative of the recent past, nor is there space or necessity here to quote every exponent.

If, indeed, the Norman Church did welcome the kind of iron-clad security which Rufus provided during his lifetime, that welcome turned into something else upon his death.

We cannot go further without touching upon motives and suspects, of both of which there were more than a few. Let us dispense first with the most lightweight and the most outlandish.

If the game were '*Cherchez la femme*', there would be two possibilities. One ancient account offers the theory of a *crime passionel.* Isabelle de Beaulieu, a ward of the Countess of Warrenne (it states) had recently been married to Walter Tirel and was Queen of the Revels at the sports arranged for the King's amusement. The King and Tirel both took part in the archery competition and the King was the most successful archer. It was here that he saw Tirel's wife for the first time, dispatched Tirel on a pretext until the following day and managed to possess the Lady Isabelle. When Tirel returned, she told him and then stabbed herself to death. The same day, Tirel, concealing the death of his wife from the King, accompanied Rufus to the hunt – and shot him.

In fact, Tirel had not recently married anybody. He had been enfeoffed into the De Clare family (which was going to bring him trouble enough, as we shall see) for some fifteen years since his marriage to Adelice (Alice), youngest sister of Earl Gilbert and Roger de Clare. Lady Alice was at Tirel's home in Ponthieu, and if there were any revels of a carnal nature they went unrecorded by scribes who were most anxious to uncover any such detail.

The other lady said to be at the root of foul play was Eadgyth, daughter of Malcolm Canmore, King of Scotland, and his Queen, Margaret, granddaughter of Edmund Ironside, an early king of the English.

Henry, youngest son of the Conqueror, already the father of several children by various mistresses, was without legal heir and his advisers urged him to marry. His fancy was for Eadgyth. Some years previously, so the story goes, Rufus himself had been so impressed by report of Eadgyth's beauty and charms that he went to see her while she was staying with her aunt, the Abbess Christina, at Romsey. The Abbess, not favouring a match between her niece and this man who was ugly as well as dissolute, dressed Eadgyth in a nun's habit and veil and sent her into the garden with other nuns. Rufus, seeing the beauty so garbed, went on his way.

Eadgyth came into the care of her aunt again when her parents died. Perhaps, says a rather coy narrator, she was living as a nun at Romsey when Henry took the throne. In any event, he lost no time in putting the case of their marriage before reinstated Bishop Anselm. An assembly of dignitaries was called and it was agreed that Eadgyth was no nun and was free to marry Henry. On November 11, three months after the Canterton killing, Eadgyth became Queen Matilda – a most popular move because her Saxon background boosted Henry's acceptance as sovereign by the English.

It seems that, at some stage, Rufus had already legislated on the matter of Matilda and had ruled that she be not allowed to leave Romsey Abbey. The suggestion is that Rufus stood in the way of Henry and his true love and that this led to his removal. But to believe that Henry, a known womaniser and an irresponsible fellow, should first gain the blessing of the conscientious Abbess Christina and then take on the cares of a kingdom purely to be able to bring Eadgyth from her cloister to his fireside is – shall we say – a bridge too far.

The most astonishing reason supplied for Rufus's death is that he, as a 'Perfect', a witch-king of the Catharist heresy, had actually willed it, regarding himself as the sacrifice necessary 'on the morrow of Lammas' to make amends for the sins of the world – the parallel term employed by those on the anti-Christian side of the dualist beliefs.

Freeman had put Rufus in parenthesis with the Devil and Margaret Murray (in her book, *God of the Witches*) went further. Rufus could, she thought, be of a line of Red Kings stretching back to the earth's oldest religion, formed in the Palaeolithic caves, when the horned king was the Sacrifice and the Wise.

Using this, the coincidence of dates and some carefully chosen ambiguities from the less reputable accounts of the killing, Hugh Ross Williamson, in *The Arrow and the Sword*, propounded a theory of consequence which had Rufus linked with the Troubadours, themselves providing the intellectual wing of the anti-Christ. In fact, the friendship of Rufus and Guilhem de Ponthieu, founding father of the Troubadours, is a matter of record but at a stage when these minstrels were poet-songsters of the highest Romantic idiom and long before there emerged any Grail motifs in their compositions.

Jack Lindsay *(The Age of the Troubadours)* suggests Rufus may have influenced Guilhem's thinking, but that is more likely a reference to debauchery along fairly orthodox lines.

An important part of HRW's argument is based on a portion of overheard conversation allegedly between Rufus and Tirel, in which the King had told the 'stranger at court' (Gaimar's phrase), 'It is right that the sharpest arrows should be given to him who knows how to give death-bearing strokes with them.' Comments Williamson: 'In the majority of accounts he is slain by an arrow loosed by his intimate, Tirel, after Tirel's hesitation and the King's command: "Shoot, in the Devil's name, or it will be the worse for you".'

If these accounts are in the majority, then this must be the silent or at least the obscure majority. None of the versions penned within striking distance of the event makes such a claim, and it is probable that the subsequent ecclesiastical adjusters were able to provide the 'proof' which HRW found so attractive.

A thought – Geoffrey Gaimar, with his elaborate rhyming 'realism', seems a far more likely Troubadour than Rufus, who was next-door to illiterate.

The Cathari, as Juanita Casey records in *The New Forest: A Symposium* (J.M. Dent & Sons Revised Edition, 1966) – and she's a Williamson fan – were highly successful as heresy goes and gave the Church a good deal of alarm. Their doctrine was a curious mixture of borrowings from Zoroaster, Mithraism, Gnosticism and Pauline teachings.

Unfortunately, they were far too late on the scene to have had much sway with William Rufus. They were second-generation Bogomils and the 'little foxes', as Eberwin, prior to the Premonstratensian House at Steinfeld, near Cologne, termed the Bogomil missionaries, did not surface in Europe until 1143.

The Cathars had no organisation, let alone credibility, in Europe until around 1145 and gained ground between then and 1170 – all the time moving further and further away from what would surely have been one of their most prestigious manifestations of faith in a clearing in the New Forest.

Eberwin it was (says R.I. Moore in *The Origins of European Dissent*) who called the 'little foxes' and their Cathari successors 'a new heresy'.

If the witch-king argument were not effectively confounded by the facts, it would fall down on the basis of logic. Rufus had been recorded as saying he would spend the Christmas of 1100 in Poitiers, and here was a man who would make pronouncements like that because his love affair was with life and not with death. The abundance and variety of his vices confirm rather than disprove that fact. His existence seems to be governed by two considerations, pleasure and profit, and he would demand one or the other from any of his ventures, physical or metaphysical. His fall, as outlined, could hardly be classed as pleasurable – and by what shall a man's death profit him?

The searchers for supernaturality cite the two versions of Rufus's burial in the sanctuary of Winchester Cathedral. While the clerical scribes insisted that no bell was rung, no mass was said, no offerings made for his soul, the poets – 'the early Troubadours', HRW points out – swore that the body was strewn with flowers and buried with 'such sayings of masses as no man had heard before or would hear again till the day of doom'.

Both sides admit that the number of people present was considerable and that may be the one piece of veracity between them. The funeral of the monarch, especially after a slaying in such circumstances, was bound to prove major box-office and whether the reality was silence or flowers does not matter a great deal . . . since neither side could be depended upon to be telling the truth.

If the death was not sacrificial, could it be assassination at grass-roots level?

The Forest had already claimed two of William's relatives – his brother, Richard, while hunting, by a pestilential blast (says William of Malmesbury) or from the effects of a blow against a tree (says Gulielmus Gemeticensis); his nephew, also Richard, either wounded by an arrow through the neck or caught by the boughs of a tree and strangled (William of Malmesbury) or killed by the arrow of one of his own knights (Orderic Vitalis and Florence of Worcester).

The latter cause tallies very closely with one account of Rufus's fall and it has been suggested that the same story was used to cover a more sinister happening in the case of Rufus. The possibility of a device is less important than the fact it was intended to hide.

Those who know the Forest well are quite happy to accept that the slayers of the two minor royal personages could well have been locals, visiting the sins of the father upon the sons or acting out of a grievance with the current administration and extreme Forest laws. But full-scale regicide, they feel, is a little too ambitious.

> 'Around the spot where erst he felt the wound,
> Red William's spectre walked his nightly round.
> When o'er the swamp he cast his blighting look,
> From the green marshes of the stagnant brook,
> The bittern's sullen shout the edyes shook;
> The waning moon, with storm presaging gleam,
> Now gave and now withheld her doubtful beam;
> The old oak stooped his arms, then flung them high,
> Bellowing and groaning to the troubled sky.'

That piece of verse, unacknowledged in W.H. Rogers' *Guide to the New Forest* (circa 1890), was said to represent admirably the way the Foresters felt about the event. And their reaction over the centuries has been important and consistent – romantic, superstitious and, even today, still a little frightened. They could not have pulled the bow that loosed the shaft. Nor do I suspect them of the earlier misadventures. The Forester personality would draw the line at anything above mischief – justified mischief, profitable mischief, pranks for which they occasionally paid very dearly. And pranks, perhaps, that might have appeared a lot more serious to those on the receiving end.

But they would have seen no advantage in killing Rufus because one king was always replaced by another and hard times could become even harder. No, the advantage lay much higher up the social scale – at the level where the gain would be direct. And immediate.

Which speaks of treason. In fact, it would be fair to say that the rule of Rufus could be marked out by milestones in treachery.

His uncle Odo, Bishop of Bayeux, spearheaded the first rebellion against him while he was still picking his most comfortable position on the throne.

William, Bishop of Durham, conspired against him.

Bishop Gosfrith and his nephew Robert, Earl of Northumberland, rebelled in the west while Roger Montgomery was busy inciting insurgence on the Welsh Marches. In the eastern counties, Roger Bigod turned his hand against the monarch; in the Midlands, Hugo of Grentemesnil was the knight in the woodpile (William of Malmesbury). And that was just the beginning.

In 1096, Rufus had cause (just or unjust) to accuse his own godfather,

William of Aldrey, of treason and send him to the gallows.

William, Count of Eu, a kinsman of Rufus, was hung on a rood, again for treason. Eudes, Count of Champagne, lost his land and others lost their eyes *(Anglo-Saxon Chronicle)*.

Roger of Yvery led a revolt of Midland barons and was forced to flee, forfeiting his vast estates close to the New Forest.

Normandy, from whence Tirel had just come (observes Wise) 'swarmed with outlawed enemies, both churchmen and laymen. It was the nest where all the plots could be safely hatched.'

And the Conqueror's son, Robert, made Duke of Normandy at his father's death-bed, a knight but no statesman, cared little to prevent that traffic, even if he had had the strength. His concerns were elsewhere, with battles he could *win* – and he always forgave his enemy once the result was assured.

Certain nobles, then, had their own reasons to wish Rufus dead – and leading churchmen had other reasons.

At the time of his death, Rufus held in his hand the Archbishopric of Canterbury, the bishoprics of Winchester and Salisbury and eleven abbacies, all bringing in handsome rents and reserves.

Certainly, by the very tone of its pronouncements, real and retrospective, the Church was aware of a clandestine arrangement to relax the monarch; but whether all ecclesiastics were agreed on the form that relaxation should take is not clear.

The sequence of dreams so carefully collated after the event and so carefully dated before it can either be the complete cover-up job or, given its most righteous interpretation, an indication that there were religious quarters so genuinely concerned for his welfare that they tried to tell him in anticipation of August 2, 1100, either to change his ways or to steer clear of the spot/action at which he would be killed . . . even if they did offer the advice in a contrived, fantastic way.

Dream No. 1 was allegedly from Rufus himself during the night of August 1/2. He dreamt that he was bled and the stream of blood, flowing up to Heaven, obscured the light of the sun.

Dream No. 2 was experienced by a foreign monk staying at the court at Malwood and brought to the King's attention by Robert Fitzhamon, one of the most trustworthy members of that hunting party. The monk dreamed he had seen the King enter a church, seize the crucifix and attempt to tear the arms and legs off. The image, after bearing the insult for some time, struck the King and felled him to the ground. Then fire and smoke gushed from the King's mouth and veiled the earth from the brightness of the stars.

Dream No. 3 was contained in a letter brought to Malwood by a monk from St Peter's Abbey at Gloucester. The letter, written by Serlo, the Abbot, told of a dream which one of the brethren had had. In his vision, the monk saw the Saviour and all the host of Heaven standing around the great white throne. Then came the Virgin Mary, robed in light, and flung herself at the feet of her Son. She prayed Him by His precious blood and agony on the Cross, to take pity on the English. She begged Him, too, as Judge of all men and avenger of all wickedness, to punish the King. Christ answered her: 'You must be patient and wait; due retribution will, in time, befall the wicked.'

Dream No. 4, recounted by Alanus de Insulis, who was not always the best authority, in fact took place some time before the other three when the banished Anselm was on a visit to Hugh, Abbot of Cluny. The abbot reported that he had seen Rufus summoned before God and sentenced to damnation and that the King's death (in vision) followed immediately. When Hugh's chaplain went to Lyons the following day, he was told twice by a youth of the death of the King before it had happened.

On the day of the slaying (though prior to it) one Peter de Melvis, in Devonshire, met a countryman who showed him a dart and said, 'With this dart, your King was killed today.' There is the report of a noble in another Forest on that day who met a black goat bearing a naked corpse. The goat told him, 'This is the body of your King.' And there is the claim that Henry, brother of Rufus, stopped for refreshment at a Forest cottage during the hunt and was hailed by an old woman as King of England.

Most tellingly, there is a most remarkable sermon preached by Fulchered, first abbot of Shrewsbury, at St Peter's Abbey on St Peter's Day, in which he bemoaned the wrongs and woes of England and concluded: 'The bow of God's vengeance is bent against the wicked. The arrow, swift to wound, is already drawn out of the quiver. Soon will the blow be struck; but the man who is wise to amend will avoid it.' (Orderic Vitalis in *Historia Ecclesiastica* and *Patrologiae Cursus*.)

For this reason and for others and to 'increase their authority with the vulgar', as Rogers puts it, the Church were pulling all the stops out to make the days sound Apocalyptic – and doing it in an Apochryphal way.

If it were a matter of apportioning corporate blame for the assassination, then our quest might not need to go any further – Church and nobility between them provide a sufficient weight of evidence based on motive, opportunity and prior intent.

Their objective was simple – to gain a sovereign who was more amenable to their suggestions, more sympathetic to their needs.

Robert was miles away. Henry was only too pleased to be involved in any scheme which would improve his presently remote chance of gaining the

English throne. It is impossible to say who was counsellor and who was dupe or even if that was the status of each party. More reasonably, it was a matter of cold-blooded negotiation between the two sides.

They reached the stage where they were ready to put out a contract for the killing. But who was the hit-man they hired?

Walter Tirel, by any definition, seems a poor choice for prime suspect. From what little is known of his history, he appears to have followed his grandfather and father in the capacity to do the right thing for his family and for his Church. A gentle kind of man who was quite liable (according to the Cartulary of Hesdun in the *Bibliothèque Nationale*) to exemplify his concern for his feudal tenants by making a free grant of houses to the village of Verton and freedom of toll to Beaurain. But a man who, quite by accident, perhaps, was good with a bow.

Malmesbury and Vitalis put the bow in Walter's hand since that is what they were told. Tirel's flight to Poole and Normandy is common to all accounts – but his reason for making it?

Wise – though he says Tirel 'certainly did not shoot the arrow' – explains the Lord of Poix's rapid return to Normandy as a clear sign that he was implicated in the plot and that he was anxious to convey news of the success of the venture.

But suppose the 'stranger at court' (Gaimar) was the only one *not* implicated in the plot.

Walter had married into the De Clare family, whose loyalties were suspect but the family member who was closest to him – Alice – was above reproach, with none of her brothers' amoral ways.

If anybody is likely to be a dupe, it may well be Tirel himself – and once the accusations started flying over the corpse, he might well have found himself embarrassingly short of friends.

Towards the end of his life, Tirel took a pilgrimage to Jerusalem – 'to expiate his share in the murder,' says Wise in pure speculation.

But, nearing death, Tirel insisted not once but several times to Abbot Suger of St Denis (recorded in Suger's *Life of Louis Le Gros*) that on the day of Rufus's death, some 35 years before, he had not only not entered that part of the Forest, but had not even seen the King; which should not be read as a blanket denial of having been with the fatal hunting party at all but simply that he had not been in the same section of woodland and, as a consequence, had not had the King in sight when the killing occurred.

These protestations were uttered at a time when most religious people, as a matter of conviction, held it necessary to make everything right with their consciences before they faced the Almighty. And the record shows Tirel to be just such a person. Furthermore, with Henry already dead – as were most of the others who had been on the spot for the fall of Rufus – there was no point in continuing with a pretence. If Tirel said he didn't do it – he didn't.

So let us consider the other members of the hunting party.

Henry, brother of Rufus. Ten years younger, rather more attractive to look upon, as witness his spectacular success with the womenfolk. Still a bachelor but the father of many children. Landless but not without cash. A fixer of the highest order who managed to keep himself free of ties.

Earl Gilbert de Clare and his brother, Roger, long-time friends of Henry. Good men to have on any side of a conspiracy.

Robert Fitzhamon, probably Rufus's oldest and closest friend. Among the few to support him against Odo and the barons in 1088 and with him again to face the Midland barons in 1095.

While one fallow buck browses on fern, his more nervous colleague moves off.

Norman barons Gilbert de Laigle and William de Montfichet, about whom little is known – which is actually a point in favour of their non-participation.

William de Breteuil, one whom the King trusted implicitly, since he gave him charge of the Treasury – cash, crown jewels and the *Liber de Thesauro*, inventory of the King's possessions in England and the collective term for the Domesday Book and its related surveys. The man who knew the score – but probably not on this occasion.

And others – court officials, huntsmen . . . and one whom Gerald of Wales, from the safe distance of sixty years, names as Ranulf de Aquis, killer of William Rufus.

The man is an enigma, a throwaway phrase, a name with which to conjure. More is known of his introducer, Gerald of Wales (Giraldus Cambrensis), Bishop of St David's, Pembrokeshire, whose reputation was for shafts of wit rather than shafts of steel.

Gerald, learned and well-travelled, was one of the two most accomplished observers – the other was Walter Mapes – to emerge from that Early Middle Age period. But while Mapes went on to make a fool of himself over the degree and dimension of the Conqueror's atrocities in his New Forest annexement, Gerald preferred to make fools of others. He was a supreme satirist whose neat turn of phrase endeared him not only to those seeking good cheer in their literature but also, allegedly, to the Pope of his time.

In his *Gemma Ecclesiastica*, he outlined the dilemma of the parish priest – a man so illiterate that he hardly knew enough Latin to repeat the services; a man so badly imbursed that he kept the money paid to him for masses; a man so prone to the desires of the flesh that he – said Gerald – 'kept a hearth-girl who kindled his fires but extinguished his virtue.'

But while scribes like Geoffrey Gaimar might have cast around for effect, Gerald found ironies enough in the situations he outlined and his reliability is unquestioned, even today.

The best satire does not go beyond the limits of good taste, but within those confines much fun can be had and Gerald had a marvellous balance when walking the line between rashness and reserve. Thus, in the late 12th century – when Suger's *Louis* and Tirel's solemn denial were factors well circulated – Gerald penned *De Instructione Principum*.

In this work he did not question the story of 'mischance' in the Canterton killing and there may well be sound editorial reasons. Apart from the racy/risque balance, such a line of inquiry might well have prompted inner questionings which he preferred not to pursue. He was, after all, a churchman not only believing in God but also in what he (Gerald) was doing. Assessing it against the 'greater good', he may well have considered no useful purpose would be served by pointing the finger at his employers . . . But he did point the finger at 'Ranulf de Aquis'.

Duncan Grinnell-Milne on whose investigation of Ranulf I have based these facts about him, ends the trail here, apart from toying with the name linguistically; and in truth perhaps it will prove there is no further to go. But I have a feeling that will not be denied and some facts which are rather stronger than coincidence, and I want to try them on one man who was among the most famous (or infamous) in England in 1100.

Ranulf de Aquis, taken literally, would mean (approximately) Ranulf of the Springs or Ranulf of the Waters.

The Ordnance Survey Sheet shows a spring rising to the east of Stoney Cross Plain, negotiating marshland south of Long Beech and then flowing on into the inclosure until it meets with Coalmeer Gutter which, in turn, runs out on to our search area. A man hailing from that spot and knowing that neck of the Forest might well connect with the Grinnell-Milne conclusion that Ranulf de Aquis was the Chief Hunter on that ill-fated expedition.

But that does not quite accord with Gerald's style. Tongue in cheek but not foot in mouth was Gerald of Wales. To my mind, 'Ranulf de Aquis' was an alias or, at least, half of one; and his position was as a chief hunter of a different kind, a hunter after revenues, a Ranulf called Flambard.

Ranulf Flambard was the most powerful man in England next to the King. He had enjoyed status for eleven years under Rufus and for some years before that under the Conqueror. He would enjoy it again under Henry.

Flambard is not mentioned by name by any of the chroniclers as being a member of the hunting party and that may be as true an indication as any that he was not there. On the other hand, so regular was his presence alongside Rufus that he might not have been suspected nor even particularly noticed.

But that is hardly a serious suggestion. More likely to me is the possibility that he was in the area without being with the party.

By 1100, Flambard was Bishop of Durham but work was hardly complete on his Christchurch Priory, which had been taking shape slowly over the last eight or nine years. It would have been perfectly natural for him to visit the Priory and to tie up that visit with some overnight sanctuary accorded to Tirel on his flight to Normandy.

Flambard as assassin? The Christchurch-Cadnam-Romsey route would have brought him within an ace of the woodland where the King was hunting and no questions asked.

No questions asked . . . Rufus fell dead without uttering a word – slain by someone he knew and trusted implicitly? The man would not even have needed to be much of a marksman at short range.

Flambard – though it adds little one way or the other – could even have fitted in with Hugh Ross Williamson's construction of the incident. According to Williamson in *The Arrow and the Sword*, he was the son of a priest and a witch, personal 'chaplain' to Rufus as well as chief minister . . . 'whose "fiery" surname had implications of the same order as Rufus's own.'

Under the dualist scheme of things, a bishop could be a 'Devil' and vice versa. Flambard, Bishop of Durham, would have been an ideal choice to carry out the sacrifice which Williamson envisages – the 'cleansing fire', in fact.

'De Aquis'? The most tenuous of links. Gerald had a way of cannibalising the Latin and French in names until it was barely recognisable, either as a means of ridicule or as an exclusively private joke. The most that can be said with certainty of 'De Aquis' is that it meant what he meant it to mean.

Perhaps it was a reference to Flambard's connection with Christchurch and the Priory which overlooked the marshland fed by two rivers, the Stour and the Avon. Or was it a token mention of his later (1101) escape from the Tower of London and down the Thames? Could it have been addressed to the rain-spouting grotesques which Flambard favoured atop his buildings? Did it take note of Flambard's 'son-of-a-witch' tag and imply that he shared his mother's alleged aversion (superstition of the time) for running water?

Flambard as assassin has the weakness of unanswered questions and speculating space. I prefer Flambard as paymaster to an unknown marksman of his own hiring or one picked out by all the conspirators. The facts reveal him better as that kind of man.

He drops out of sight between 1097, when he is installed at Durham, and 1101 when he is stripped of his possessions and imprisoned in the Tower of London during a visit to England by Robert Curthose, eldest son of the Conqueror. But the Tower does not a prison make for Flambard, because he helped to design it. With deceptive ease, he makes his escape down the Thames and surfaces again in Normandy in 1103, apparently on some kind of secret service for Henry. By 1107, he is back again as Bishop of Durham, with even more possessions than he had when Henry 'deprived' him.

These are the bare facts and perhaps they could benefit from a little more meat, but to me they make a certain kind of sense.

Henry has deliberately initiated no kind of inquiry into his brother's death and when Robert turns up, perhaps demanding such an investigation, my prime suspect is taken out of circulation – not a serious attempt at imprisonment because Flambard knows the Tower like the back of his hand and Henry knows that he knows.

In 1103, Flambard is perfectly happy to be serving the man who benefited most from the death of his master.

In September, 1106, Henry and Robert meet in battle at Tinchebrai, Henry conquers Normandy and Robert ends his days as a prisoner in a jail not so easy to slip. Flambard goes back in triumph to Durham – and it is difficult to resist the thought that this is payment for the intelligence he had fed back to Henry from Robert's troubled duchy of Normandy and for his undercover part in the Curthose downfall.

Flambard, from the way he conducts his affairs, emerges as a survivor – a man who gives his second loyalty to his monarch but his first loyalty to himself . . . but a man whose second loyalty is so spectacular that unstable kings and princes are happy to settle for it.

Conclusions: perhaps the mistake we make these days is in applying our own standards to that distant period when savagery was the rule and exceptions were not plentiful.

A clear and convincing indication of the mediaeval nuances comes not from an historian in the accepted sense but from novelist George Shipway, who makes his contribution to the Tirel/Rufus tie-up via two books, *The Paladin* and *The Wolf Time*. He is eager to admit – in a preliminary note to *The Wolf Time* – that his researches have shed no new light on the murder, that he has taken what he can from the chroniclers and invented the rest. But it is an invention based on rather more than the Canterton affair – an extrapolation of the rule of force as outlined by all the best factual accounts.

His reconstruction of the killing is valuable not just because it rings as true as good steel and, for that reason, could be exact. It takes its real merit from the easy-come-easy-go atmosphere which prevails throughout.

Life is hard and, as a consequence, death is ever at hand. If somebody blocks the path to your goal, there is one short way of removing him. Kill or be killed. Above all, cover your tracks – or get the monks to do it for you. That was the state of the world on August 2, 1100, when William Rufus closed his eyes upon it. The manner of his death and the manner of the cover-up that overlapped it on either side were formalities which became puzzles only when the commentators got to work.

The power of the media is not a 20th century phenomenon. Nothing, you might say, could be further from the truth.

State versus Lisle

A crow following the sunset from Canterton in a straight line would cross the grounds of red-brick Moyles Court (now a private school) and put down upon a memorial stone, of a very different kind from Rufus's, in the churchyard of St Mary and All Saints at Ellingham.

No time of day can be a bad time for approaching the beauty of that churchyard, but I venture to suggest that the time of year we went there would take some beating. It was late May, with the sun already giving us a hint of what June and July could be like. The approach, after a left turn off the Ringwood-Fordingbridge road (A338) was between high banks lush with long grasses and dense in cow parsley.

St Mary and All Saints and the serenity that surrounds it are as good an explanation as I have ever found of how Thomas Gray came to write his elegy. If it is the existence of death in the midst of life that provides the sting, then perhaps the balm that comes to life in the midst of death is a matter of metaphysical balance.

First contact is with the gate, remarkable not for the design but for the care lavished on it. The wood has not only been stained but varnished lovingly so that your fingers come away with a warmth rather than a splinter. This, if you like, is the handshake, and it sets you up for the rest of the encounter. There is a temptation to lean your arms on this warmth and go no farther, to keep the little church and its grounds as a treat in store while a peacock calls from somewhere beyond the whitewashed house on your right.

It is the kind of scene and the kind of sound that makes moments precious, with the yew and hedgerow rustling and the swifts making traceries around the tower with its one Clement Tosier bell.

But we came with a definite purpose and there is a limit to what we can see from here. The delights out of sight may yet be greater.

The herbage about the graves is long enough to bear daisies and lesser celandines but short enough to be respectable and paths trimmed to a smoothness run hither and thither. On the western side, parterres surround the Earls of Normanton and their ladies and a separate border marks the grave of the lady who was nanny to the Normanton family for 56 years.

From this point, you can peer through the laurel bushes and down into the adjoining farm, which boasts a huge thatched barn – almost as much straw on the roof as inside – and a shed for just about every modern device . . . as well as a ford in the middle of the yard. There cannot be many farms which strive to capture a part of the Avon stream for a duckpond, but here it goes, ripple, ripple, under a five-bar gate and off again across yellow meadows.

You cannot hold water. And you cannot hold time, but here at St Mary and All Saints they do favour Nature above the chronometer in recording its passage.

The vertical sundial, blue and gilded in the triangular tympanum above the 1720 porch was working most wonderfully when we visited. In 1930, the Rev. Charles Wesley Darling tested the accuracy of the sundial readings with the Royal Observatory at Greenwich and discovered that, after correction for longitude and the equation of time, the readings were five minutes 35 seconds too small. Checking the shadows against my wrist, I found that the difference was small indeed.

The letters 'J.M.' cut into the porch are the initials of James Mist, churchwarden, who was possibly its donor. About two yards to the east we found the chest tomb that had brought us to Ellingham. 'Here lieth Dame Alicia Lisle and her daughter Ann Harfell, who dyed the 17th of Feb 1709/8' – a curious flat-topped symbol now looking like an upside-down, inverted 2 – 'Alicia Lisle dyed the second of Sept. 1685.'

It is only recently that the stone has been cleaned, showing the figures more clearly. When it was covered with ivy, it was reported by the *Gentleman's Magazine* in 1828 as unreadable. Brian Vesey-Fitzgerald, in his *Portrait of the New Forest*, made it 1702. The church register, the only record of Ann's death, gives the date as 1708.

Her name too was hard to read, and 'Ann Hortell' was that writer's version, while 'Anne Hartell' (John R. Wise, 1883) and 'Agnes Harfell' (Joan Begbie, 1934) are to be found in other books.

All this is a small matter, perhaps. But half truths are fitting in connection with this particular tomb, for it holds also the body of Alicia Lisle, the venerable mistress of Moyles Court, who was tried and executed for harbouring John Hickes after the Monmouth Rebellion. And, while much has been written about this sad affair, it is founded on records which are scant in the extreme.

Very basically, what happened was this: Dame Alicia, aged 71 and known to be a woman of Christian charity, was asked by a man called Dunne to give shelter to two rebels, John Hickes and Richard Nelthorp, running for their lives after the Battle of Sedgemoor had brought an end to the Duke of Monmouth's aspirations to the throne. (She was never tried for harbouring Nelthorp.)

Dame Alicia was not, so she said, aware that Hickes (a dissenting minister), had been in the battle; only that he was a man trying to make his own way with God. She was also not aware of Nelthorp's name, let alone his complicity in the rebellion.

Dunne, having placed his charges in her care, then alerted one Colonel Penruddock, who was on the look-out for dissidents to bring them to trial. And Penruddock, whose father, it was said, had been sentenced to death by Dame Alicia's late husband, Lord Lisle, 30 years before, went straightway to Moyles Court and arrested the two fugitives and Dame Alicia with them. (A fresco which decorates the corridor of the House of Commons is E.M. Ward's version of the scene of the arrest and is as good a representation as any that exists.)

Dame Alicia, taken to Winchester, was tried by Judge Jeffreys at the start of his 'Bloody Assizes' and sentenced to pay the penalty for high treason, which was burning alive, 'this very afternoon'. But, for some reason buried in the morass of conflicting accounts, a stay of execution was secured so that Dame Alicia could petition James II for clemency.

According to Henry Muddiman, newswriter at the office of Lord Middleton (a Secretary of State at the time) and one of the few commentators who did not have an axe to grind, the King 'mitigated the sentence of burning her alive to the severing (of) her head from her body.' Muddiman adds: 'On the 2nd. (of September) about 4 in the afternoon, Mrs. Lisle was beheaded at Winchester. They give not anything of remarks upon the scaffold but that she was old and dozy and died without much concern.'

The real tragedy was not that she should become a victim of Judge

Jeffreys but that she should have become involved in the political situation at all. At Ellingham today, it is still easy to understand that here, of all places, was a setting remote from the strife of the times. It is possible, even probable, that Sedgemoor meant nothing to Dame Alicia, since the communication of news had a lot to do with the efforts of a fast horse.

But the story of Dame Alicia Lisle, elaborated through the troubled years after her death, is one tangled with political motives. Add to it the publication of her alleged 'dying speech', a forgery perpetrated (for his own good reasons) by one John Tutchin, and quite alien to the character of an 'old, dozy' woman approaching her dotage, and the best thing that can be done is to wish peace to an old lady better left to make her own twilight way to this stone chest in Ellingham churchyard.

But what happened to Dame Alicia once at the church is still a matter of some doubt. The church's extremely able historian, Dr R.H. Little, thinks it doubtful that she would have been buried inside the building when she was a convicted felon, however questionable the trial might have been. His predecessor, the Rev. Charles Wesley Darling, however, thought that the body might have been inside the church at one time, and he left a note to that effect: 'Alice Lisle was beheaded in 1685 but the stone of her tomb was not engraved till after the death of her daughter, Mrs Ann Harfell, in 1708. The stone is not dressed round the edges which looks as if it was intended to be placed in the floor of the church. The stone rested on brick walls at one time but about 1850 the present stone walls were substituted.'

Perhaps the question will never be resolved. Perhaps it has little consequence anyway, because by the end of September, 1689, Dame Alicia's status no longer bore any stigma. Some months after William of Orange and Queen Mary followed James II to the throne, they sanctioned an Act of Parliament which had arisen as a result of a petition from two more of Dame Alicia's daughters, Tryphena Lloyd and Bridget Usher.

Said the Act: 'Whereas Alicia Lisle, widow . . . by an irregular and undue procedure was indicted for entertaining, concealing and comforting John Hickes, clerk, a false traitor, knowing him to be such, though the said John Hickes was not at the trial of the said Alicia Lisle attainted or convicted of any such crime, and by a verdict injuriously extorted and procured by the menaces and violences and other illegal practices of George, Lord Jeffreys, Baron of Wem, then Lord Chief Justice, etc., was convicted, attainted and executed for High Treason . . . May it please your most excellent Majesties . . . that the said conviction and judgment and attainder of the said Alicia Lisle be . . . repealed, reversed, made and declared null and void . . . and that no corruption of blood, or other penalty, or forfeiture of her own dignities, lands, goods or chattels be by the said conviction incurred, etc.'

William of Orange, a favourite of the Whigs, had not been inactive in the machinations which had led to the downfall and death of his father-in-law, James II, and in the circumstances such a recompense was a small price to pay. Dame Alicia Lisle had been far more use to him dead than alive . . .

Inside the church itself, we are reminded that Brian Vesey-Fitzgerald had found here evidence of a caring congregation. He had remarked on the modern strip lighting and storage heaters, while I would cite something a little more intricate – like 100 stitches to the square inch; like Tent, Cross, Long-Legged Cross, Montenegrin, Eye, Rice, Satin Diagonal, Satin Padded, Back, Mosaic, Fern, Knotted, Flat, Parisian and Florentine; from all of which you will know that I am speaking of embroidery. A team of 22 needlewomen took about five years to complete runners for the 26 pews of the church nave, each one worked with the symbol of the saints – and some of the saints, one might add, of the lesser-known variety: Kentigern, Matthias, Aidan, Edmund, Simon Zelotes. These runners were quite apart from the kneelers and cushions created in between times.

Such evidence of industry, and alongside it, in the middle of it, such an atmosphere of peace.

When we retraced our steps to the gate, the peacock was still calling and the only embroiderers in view were the swifts mending holes in the blue sky. The gate which had been warm was now cool to our hot touch, changing its service as we had changed our demands – from 'Welcome' to a cordial 'Au revoir'.

It seemed, indeed, a place most fitted to accommodate sad Dame Alicia Lisle – a gentle, declining lady far more fitted to embroidery than to imbroglio.

Place of Beauty

TO most people, Beaulieu is the motor museum, the folk festival, the one-way village that runs out of parking places by very early a.m. None of them would ever think of calling it sleepy. Serve them right for coming in summer.

In 1778, Lord Lyttelton of Cobham Hall was complaining: 'Coaches full of travellers of all denominations, and troups of holiday neighbours, are hourly chasing me from my apartment or strolling about the environs keeping me a prisoner in it. The lord of the place can never call it his during the finest part of the year.' Nearly 200 years later (in his book *The Gilt and the Gingerbread*, 1966) Lord Montagu of Beaulieu was happy to direct the Lyttelton comment to the plight of the stately home owner in the late 20th century – although since, it must be said, he has reconciled himself handsomely to living with the phenomenon.

But arrive as we did, in a season of fair weather when the days of March were still in single figures, and you would be taken immediately with the exquisite lassitude and peace of spirit that gained this riverhead the name of Bellus Locus (place of beauty) when King John had a hunting lodge here, circa 1199. From the Latin it was but a short step to the French – 'Beau Lieu' – and nothing lost in the translation.

The Cistercian monks from the manor of Farringdon who moved in at John's behest in 1204 must have blessed the bad dream (according to tradition) or the concession under an entente engineered by the Archbishop of Canterbury between king and Cistercians (according to history) which brought them this paradise for more than 300 years.

We, in turn, blessed the sun and the unseasonal warmth and the quiet river which seemed to flow up from the sea past Salternshill, Bucklers Hard, the copses of Keeping, Spearbed and Oxley, clearing its throat of salt as it came to rest, clear and obedient, at our feet.

Rest was the theme of the day, certainly along the riverbank. Mallard and kittiwake lay down together like lion and lamb or balanced effortlessly on one leg, their heads buried beneath natural eiderdowns. The world breathed in, breathed out and was content. Across the water, we could see gabled, red-brick houses whose lawns ran down for ever to paddle their toes. And in those houses, perhaps, other folk looked out upon the serenity (for which, in truth, they had paid a very great deal) and wondered how they might order the rest of their lives without stirring from the spot.

It is not recorded whether the seagulls taught the ducks the leisure to live here or whether the lessons went the other way. But they both know the secret now.

Perhaps it is something human in the nature of the gulls that makes some of them act like shop stewards when the rest are quite happy not to think at all of productivity deals. In a little while, when the peace had become too heavy for their high strings, a militant minority took off towards Carpenters' Dock and settled *en masse* on ripples that might have meant fish to the imaginative. There they commenced a peculiarly kittiwake kind of therapy that involved no more activity than had been entailed on the bank – but at least it was free of ducks.

Two mallard, meanwhile, picked their way daintily down to the river, scooping water and then arching necks to let the liquid dribble slowly to its destination.

Two doves dropped in – one white, one of milk-chocolate mottle – pecked at the earth, sampled the water and were gone even as a gull announced his personal objection to their presence.

All the drinking was giving us a thirst, and pure though the riverhead might be, it wasn't quite what we needed. Instead, we took the bridge at an easy pace, filed singly along the narrow pavement past the Beaulieu Arms Hotel and found a tearoom that must once have enjoyed an appeal of a slightly different kind. It was at the back of a bookshop and history was at the back of the tearoom – a blackleaded three-storey oven of spectacular proportions, a tribute to Thomas Collins & Co., Engineers of Bristol. For

Beaulieu Village runs out of parking places in the summer.

Buckler's Hard – down-river from Beaulieu.

their fame – and their installation staff – to have travelled this far across Southern England would have made the job memorable indeed.

And perhaps the baking of R. & F. Stevens had been similarly auspicious. The oven had still been in use in the 1940s, we discovered from a young lady for whom the 1940s must have been like the Dark Ages. But I remember how the 1940s went in my own local bakery down a Roath, Cardiff, lane. I used to watch in wonder as a regular harp of wires produced a loaf that was already sliced and wrapped in wax-paper. If I had known then what the sliced-loaf concept was going to do to bread, perhaps my thoughts would have been more of sabotage than of awe.

I'll wager R. & F. Stevens had no harp of wires.

Now the tearoom is one of the Montagu Ventures (of which there are more than a few) and today, the bread came by van – not Sunpride or Mother's Blest, it's true, but it made us smile a little wryly as we ate our teacakes. Nice as they were . . . Nice as everything was about the Beautiful Place on that blue and gentle March day which brought out the crocus in us .

The Lights of Ringwood

THE other day – or so it seems – you could pop with us out of the Verwood turn-off, scuttle across two lanes of bypass and thread your way into Ringwood via the Market Square.

Not any more. Now a statement in red brick bars the way. 'The Berlin Wall', the locals call it and to such good effect that, in 1978, they got the Ministry to order it lowered by up to a foot in places. It was a hollow victory and not my kind of compromise at all because the Berlin Wall is not so much high as long.

The other day – or so it seems – as we motored through the square and down the High Street towards the Christchurch road, my wife used to take a deep breath somewhere between the Ringwood Bookshop (on our right) and Street's toyshop (on our left) and say, 'I *like* Ringwood.'

Or – it being a Sunday night – we might bide a while with the windows down and listen to the folk music coming from the bar of the Red Lion.

Not any more. These days, it's a turn off to the left here, third out of Roundabout No. 1, second out of Roundabout No. 2 and follow some more red-brick walling behind the village centre along a road which takes you all too soon over the hump of the old level crossing and away. Which is missing a great deal . . . in particular, two leading lights.

The Victorian street-lamp in the market square was considered to be so representative of the village that it figured in an extremely artistic plate produced for the Queen's Silver Jubilee. The lamp-post was famous not only for the illumination it cast but for the support it provided to bicycles – there to be sold on market days and just for purchase on other days as riders leant or shopped or gossiped. When the lamp's significance passed from convenience to character, the device was railed around – which didn't bother the cyclists at all. The inflated circumference gave them more room for their machines plus something to which to attach their locking chains.

It is this lamp, too, that makes a Christmas Eve in Ringwood distinctive from any other in the New Forest area. With its light supplemented by candle-power creepers of red and blue, it serves as central to the community carol-singing which gives warmth in sub-zero temperatures, sweetness above the automobile growls from the nearby trunk road, a rural setting for Royal David's City and a memorableness to all matters.

But it isn't our favourite Ringwood lamp.

On a damp November evening with the mist coming off the Avon, we discover that blue can be a warm colour, friendly in a way far more nostalgic than any jubilee . . . and no less Victorian, as I found out.

The lamp that spells out 'R-I-N-G-W-O-O-D' for us is set on iron stanchions above the gate to the police station. Its effect is greater than can be achieved by any mere bulb. In the dark and shrouded hours it glows, and that must comfort an awful lot of local people, even as it rallies us after a long journey through night.

Every police station should have one. Every police station did have one – and something happened, I think, to the way people felt about law and order when most of those lamps went out.

Not wanting to butt in upon any crises – wasting police time is an offence, you know – I waited for a quiet day and rang Ringwood Police.

'This is a rather peculiar inquiry,' I said.

'Oh, we get a lot of those,' said the cheery spokeswoman at the other end.

I asked how long the lamp had been there.

'Well, I've been here about as long as anybody – 17 years – and I never remember it any different,' she said. 'I know who could probably tell you' – and she gave me a name.

'I don't suppose there are any plans to remove it or anything terrible like that?'

'No – Well, perhaps they wouldn't tell me because I'm only the telephonist. But . . . No. I think you could say that as long as there's a police station here, there'll be a blue lamp.'

In that, I found a positively moist-eyed reassurance.

Street lamp and gathering place – the Victorian throwback which is so much more than a relic at Ringwood.

The name I had been given was that of Dr R.H. Little, historian of considerable local standing. I put the question to him.

'The police station was built in 1851,' he said without hesitation. 'I can only assume that the lamp was installed at that time.'

And how many times in 130 years, I wonder, have people seen it and thought: 'Goodnight, all . . .'

I *like* Ringwood – even if the planners have tried to make me pass by on the other side.

If you are planning a visit, choose Wednesday. And if you can follow the right signs into the (free) car park, find your way into the market place and only see the poppies when you look at the inner side of the barrier that seals off the hubbub beyond, you will come upon the proceedings much as they have been for centuries.

I have always been a push-over for street markets. There is something undeniably romantic about the vans that move into cobbled streets at dawn, drop their tailboards and throw out rainbows of silk and satin, acres of cheap shoes, Aladdin stalls of glass and brass that can be guaranteed to yield a genuine antique or two, if you look carefully. And at the end of the day, these Armenians with accents from Millwall and Merseyside wrap up their treasures and are gone.

There is all of that about Ringwood Market – plus the foam rubber stalls, the jeaneries, the racks of anoraks.

But this hub of the Forest – not the capital, for that is Lyndhurst and quite a different proposition – adds a country touch . . . vegetables as attractive in price as they are in appearance, eggs from chickens that range wide as well as free, and an auction, the like of which you will not have seen in a thousand journeyings.

Again, the whole thing revolves around that omnipresent Victorian street-lamp, and a caravan that has not felt the tug of internal combustion for some time now but serves as a snackbar. Normally, it rests upon the cobbles of the square. But on market days the proprietor and several other worthies take it by the tail and swing it to a new site in the shadow of the parish church. With the tea-counter moved, Woolley and Wallis, auctioneers, wheel in their own device for the laying of bids and the casting of lots. At the let-down flap of their on-site office, you may name your reserve or go, when bidding is done and yourself the victor, to claim and pay for your gain.

Ranged in strictly linear formation across the cobbles are the items on offer, each marked with a cloakroom ticket which has its twin with the country gentleman at the mobile H.Q. Invariably, the line-up has a flotsam look, as though some dry tide has rolled across the surrounding farmland

Ringwood Market on a rainy day.

and down the Avon to lay its scour of saw blades, old china, knock-up furniture and decadent bicycles upon this cobble shore.

A beautiful and freshly-painted gypsy caravan fashioned in wood when the work was done and land and cattle were resting; a cardboard box shared by a leatherbound collection of old sermons and a cruet where salt and pepper traces have agreed on a uniform grey; plates unashamedly cracked and 78 r.p.m. records which are not, bundled together in a tattered brown suitcase; a hedge-trimmer; a cart-wheel; a bicycle chain and a pair of handlebars; 20 parts of a 24-volume medical encyclopaedia whose owner has gone beyond sickness; a vintage Singer sewing-machine whose gold-leaf motif is decidedly autumnal; a walking stick and an umbrella lashed together, looking more forsaken than for sale. And three score and ten other lots, not one of which comes without a story – and very few of which linger where they have been placed. Ringwood market-goers love their memories . . . and the memories of other people, too.

I had an inkling once to buy a bicycle and thought this auction the ideal place to make the connection. I fixed on a model that was a good deal less than grand and appeared to have a good chance of going for the kind of price I could afford.

When the bidding got above £15, I was so breathless that I just stood back and watched. The machine's face value was left well behind; it went eventually for £27 . . . and convinced me that the normal trade of worth and potential mattered little in these circles. These items carried with them a respect and this was reflected in the offers that won them.

For something mechanical, that peculiar status brings an upward spiral. For something ornamental, the opposite seems to be true. One day, we came upon six glass fruit-dishes and their larger mother-plate, beautifully engraved from the underside with apples, pears and grapes. They had come from an old lady's cottage, said the stallholder. She was afraid they were quite expensive – £4.

In five years we have seen no workmanship as good and items of lesser artistry are fetching £60–£70 *each* in the best stores of the Sandy City.

It seems that an economy geared to usefulness is the order, and this is the kind of unchangeability – the feet planted tree-trunk firm in the good old artisan values that have motivated the New Forest for a lot longer than nine centuries – that will outlast any 'Berlin Wall', however high, however wide.

The Lost Tribe

WHERE a weatherworn caravan rests in a quiet corner of a field at Burley Street; where the Forest heaves itself free of woodland and then drops away towards the donkey zone of Godshill, Woodgreen and Breamore, there may still be a gypsy.

But I couldn't find one. My quest led me from a treasure house on a hillside far from the Forest to a deserted inclosure, a voice through a letter box, a chicken wire fence and two graveyards before I had to admit that now the travellers are all in books, under the ground or perhaps only visible to the colourful people who entertained me at the outset in that hillside house.

Which is a good place to begin . . .

Sven Berlin would be most reluctant to concede that he had offered anything to the New Forest. As far as he is concerned, the traffic in influences was all the other way. But – while the metaphor lasts – let us say that he has provided at least two vehicles of understanding in books and probably a couple of hundred more in substance if we can read the whorls and ridges of paintings and sculptures carried out while he and his caravanserai rested at Puck's Pits, at Shave Green, at Emery Down.

Now, after two attempts to return to residency – one cottage at Lepe and another inland were twitched from his fingers via the none-too-gentle art of gazumping – he has taken the evidence as signifying destiny and lives, happy only in his immediate surroundings, on the hillside above Stanbridge, near Wimborne.

He takes what life brings him. As he wrote in *Dromengro* (1971): 'It seems more evident each day that our near-future is blue-printed quite a time before it is created. Each moment is indicative of that which will happen as surely as it is of the past; there is probably no division, anyway.'

Elsewhere in *Dromengro*: 'The late E.L. Grant-Watson has written that . . . the imprint of organs as yet unborn is seen in the growing chrysalis of the butterfly. I believe this can happen also in a growing boy; he carries the organs that are to become his heritage and his destiny; they will become real experience and be given form by life and by art during the painful struggle that goes with each metamorphosis. Their imprint is a prophecy.'

'Predestination' is rather a slick word for this kind of philosophy. In that term, you know where you are going. In Sven Berlin's understanding, it is only after the event that you realise how the vagaries of life have led you unerringly to it.

And then away from it. Berlin tried once to go back to his well-loved Shave Green when the compound was in decline – not that it had ever been anything else as long as the gawjo held the reins and you needed a permit even to be there – only to find that he, who had been prala (brother) to the Coopers, the Wellses, the Lees and the Smiths was now the gawjo, the outsider.

He traced a few friends to Thorney Hill and to the cemetery. He spent good years in Devon with his new wife, Julia, daughter of former New Forest huntsman Harry Lenthall, and bad years in the Isle of Wight. Fairly recently, with the island cottage gone, he was relieved of another dwelling he had earmarked in the Forest because, he admits, 'I am afraid I am no good at business.'

But a friend had a house near Wimborne – and here, he and the fair Julia sit, surrounded by their art and seldom to be persuaded from the spacious rooms which are still a novelty after the restrictions of wagon, hut, cottage. 'Once, I used to go to the pubs,' said Sven, 'but I can't find any atmosphere in these places down the road. I look around for faces to sketch and there aren't any. It was like that on the Island.'

But it does not signify that the artist is going through an arid patch. On the Island, he produced a book called *Amergin*, which he subtitled 'An enigma of the Forest'. He wrote the first draft in five days and then set about with a sculptor's style, smoothing edges, polishing, breathing music into the marble. That took the rest of his five insular years.

Now that he can look back upon the pattern which has emerged, he sees that the book is far more than a lyrical allegory with a familiarity of setting. It is a statement of everything he ever felt about the Forest, a story on two levels which communicates in fiction to the lay reader and in factual terms to the person who knows that little bit more about Sven Berlin and his 'Great Forest in the South', with its Lone Woman Moor, its Lime Hole River and the Island of Cows in the blue distance. More than that, it is his final statement on the Forest because the duende (Romany word for spirit) and he have parted company, he claims. If he went back now, he says, he would be bound to find disappointment. There is a stage when memories are the best you can expect.

But Berlin is ahead of other men who have lived in the Forest all their lives and operate there still because he *felt* the spirit; he *knew* it.

His Julia, too. It is all tied up with experiences for which 'memory' is too soft a word. Benny Wells, voiceless and toothless with cancer in the throat, giving his last silver coins to her – 'as though', says Berlin, 'he gave his soul into her safe-keeping' – Benny admitted Julia into the life-and-death circle around which Sven already revolved, the pulse that kept working when the heart had long stopped.

And Julia may well have been a Forest intimate a lot earlier than that. Her father, Harry Lenthall, was the New Forest huntsman and in *Dromengro* Berlin relates the incident which gave birth to a legend and death to the literal Jesse Wells, whom we shall meet along the way.

Old Jesse, the deer harbourer, seeing that a hunted stag had run itself to a standstill and that the pursuing dogs were about to tear it to shreds, leapt on its back and killed it humanely with a knife. But in so doing, he did himself no good. The Huntsman, the whipper-in and the foot-followers were present as the Master bawled out Jesse for robbing him of the climax.

Berlin writes: 'Except for one beautiful unknown girl with golden hair and blue eyes on a fine horse, which she rode like a goddess, none of the gentry were (sic) in at the kill.' It is a worthwhile bet that Julia was the golden-haired girl of that instance – and it cannot be denied that she slips in and out of Berlin's dreams and realities.

'We married when I was fifty and she was nineteen,' says Sven proudly, 'and people had their doubts – although not those who knew us at all well.' That was sixteen years ago and Julia is still happy to be there, knowing Sven's recollections better than he does himself – in fact, she corrects him. So that all of it, if it were not shared before, is certainly shared now.

Julia even has her stature in Sven's literature. If the itinerant Dwyffid of his *Amergin* is modelled on himself – and the biographical facts would not gainsay it – then the Marie Louise of the piece, carrying the name of Berlin's mother, also carries the presence of his wife. If Julia and Marie Louise are not one and the same, then they are twins of Siamese proximity – and I cite the full-length portrait on the Berlin's living-room wall as conclusive proof.

The house at Stanbridge bears ample evidence of the way Sven Berlin makes his living. The ash-trays are more likely to hold screwed-up paint-tubes than cigarettes. Wall-paper would be an affront to his own powers of decor. But not all the artwork on show is his – far from it.

Julia paints in the primitive style. Her birds and fish populate sills and alcoves and at the stop of the stairs is a bed headboard decorated with a peacock version of the Eden episode. 'After the Fall,' I say and Julia laughs nervously, as though secretly pleased that I have seen so much in the picture. Her favourite is the starling because he is friendly. She sees him studded with diamonds.

Sven quotes Pablo Picasso, approximately: 'When I was a young man, I could paint like Raphael. It took me sixty years to learn how to paint like a child.'

'The secret of the true primitive artist,' he explains, 'is that he – or she – never loses that ability. Julia never lost it; only found it.'

Because Sven Berlin now feels that his links with the New Forest are broken, does he still have a validity in our context?

To my mind, yes. In metaphysical terms, he is no less of an archivist than David Stagg, though his stock in trade is Muse rather than manuscript. He, it is (and mostly through *Amergin*) who gives the Forest the mystical personality which comes closest to articulating those emotions which you feel but you cannot explain.

The other records have dates on them or about them, which means that they express time. But time is a dimension which matters very little to trees which carry their years like Methuselah, and to peat bogs where the remote past is measured in depths of metres.

Sven Berlin encompasses no time and all time, intangibles and unchangeables. And if it happens that he and Julia are pinned down in Wimborne or Cornwall or East Cowes for the rest of their days, it doesn't matter. The spokesman has done his job.

For Sven Berlin, the gypsy story had ended at Shave Green. I went there to look for a beginning, for some indication that even a gawjo could recognise.

But the tracks on the earth, such as they were, came from caterpillars and not caravans. In this 'ancient and ornamental' of oak and silver birch, there were plenty of glades where a family might have pitched a tan or parked a vardo. But walk as I might, with each step tugging and black oozing patterns marking my progress, there were only the titmice to tell me; and very soon a growing roar put me in touch with the M27 and more urgent travels.

I had a suspicion that Shave Green, coming within a fence-width of the motorway, might show it in some ecological way. Boughs blackened with petrol fumes, I pictured in my doomwatch mind. All wildlife fled. A corpse instead of a copse beside the tarmac . . . Well, that hasn't happened yet. The spoors of pony and deer show that life goes on despite all. On my visit, a faint green mist played about the birches, first breath of new foliage.

It was a revelation of mixed value. The planners who had argued that nature would survive had made it sound hollow and unconvincing. And yet here I stood amid new growth, my argument lost. Ah, well. The comfort was in the truth and not the principle.

From Shave Green, switchback lanes between tall hedges with primrose toes brought me by a back way to the village of Minstead, which lies just below the site of Malwood Hunting Lodge, where Rufus ate his last meal. A final lane took me up to the church.

The most famous grave in Minstead churchyard lies to the right at the far end, and is marked by a Celtic cross. Here is buried Sir Arthur Conan Doyle, philosopher, soldier, adventurer, man of letters, who brought this village into his book, *The White Company*, and lived near Cadnam, at Bignell Wood. But now, in search of gypsy history, I was following the leftward curve of the path from the lych-gate until I reached five simple graves, no more than mounds of earth, where the most formal adornment was a vase inscribed 'In Loving Memory' and decked with daffodils and anemone. But there were no names anywhere. Two vases of orange plastic reflected the daffodil sentiment of Romany mourners who are never seen to come and yet keep the flowers fresh and the grass short by hand and not by implement.

But the mourners were thoroughly visible on a day in the early 1950s when one of these mounds was but a raw and gaping hole in the ground, waiting for Jesse Wells.

Jesse, as Sven Berlin has told, was the deer harbourer so enamoured with his charges that he would follow them for days, watching their welfare, absorbing their habits. Time and again (as Juanita Casey also records), his family, perturbed at his absence, would trace him to a hollow in the grass, soaked in dew and stiff in every joint. Jesse would stay with them long enough to take soup and thaw out. Then he would be gone again.

On the last morning of his life, he had revealed the darker side of the harbourer's coin – the service that he does for the huntsman. He had spiked the chase with a buck worth the effort.

By the time the deer had circled back through stream and plantation to the place of his precipitation, the animal was bleeding externally and internally, in agony from the pressure of the hounds. The huntsman was too

Minstead Church: burial place of Sir Arthur Conan Doyle and Jesse Wells.

far behind to shoot him. The dogs were closing and would swarm upon him like rats, tearing flesh and dignity.

Jesse found him with a broken leg, making a last effort to immerse his scent in a stream, dying but not fast enough to defy the canine descent. The old man leapt upon his back and severed his jugular veins. Then Jesse wavered.

The hunt crowd found him sitting under a tree cleaning his knife and awaiting their wrath. It surely came. And went. And a short while later, still under the tree, Jesse closed his eyes.

A nation of gypsies appeared in the Forest for his funeral, recalls Berlin. And in the sunlight, in the grounds of the little Saxon church, Jesse's red-haired daughters pushed aside the bearers and took the lowering ropes themselves, wailing as they committed him to the cold earth. They wailed for his passing – and the estrangement which had sprung up for reasons no one could remember and had not ended when it was too late to make peace.

On a previous visit to this churchyard, I had met among the graves a grey-haired and distinguished gentleman who had led me to Jesse's barrow and

'Steel true, Blade straight' – Sir Arthur Conan Doyle's gravestone.

told me of a former gypsy who had taken a Minstead roof over his head. And at the post office, the presiding foreigner (from Romsey) had told me why the Trusty Servant across the green, once a gypsy pub, no longer welcomes the gentlemen of the road.

It was on this green, in fact, that the *personae* became *non grata* when the Coopers had invited their rivals, the Witchers, from Hythe for a night on the grog and a little settlement to follow. At stop-tap, they faced each other across the green, men, women, and older children. Each side had its field-marshal, the patriarch of the family, and between them Cooper Senior and Witcher Senior singled out protagonist and opponent.

By midnight, when the match had become rather excitable and the bottles were getting more than occasional, somebody had sent for the police at Pikes Hill, five minutes away in a fast car.

Well, the police left it for half an hour so that the word could get around and the battlers could make their retreat. By the time they arrived, the war was as remote as a bad dream. But it finished the Trusty Servant as a gypsy pub. Now the Needies pass straight by the door.

But the former gypsy with the roof over his head – where was he? Today I would seek him out. So I descended from the churchyard into Minstead, a village which straggles a little, with thatched cottages and honeysuckle trailing up narrow byways, and at its centre a triangular green with the post office and general store on one side, the Trusty Servant on the second and some of the most delightful council houses to be seen anywhere, any time, on the third side. At the post office they directed me to a council house overlooking the rising meadows which surround the village, but warned me that my ex-gypsy was probably to be found in the Servant.

The front garden was tidy and uncluttered, well stocked in daffodils. My first knock brought no response.

'I think he's out,' said the man next door. 'But one of the children should be there.'

The former traveller, it seemed, had been left to look after four young while his wife headed for a better horizon. My churchyard informant had told me that in Silver Jubilee Year the village had prepared a list of children to receive commemorative mugs. The organisers knew the list was incomplete and that the gypsy chavis were the missing ones. A polite inquiry had revealed that their father wasn't able to add the names to the list, but, soon enough, somebody had done it for him.

My second knock sparked a lengthy ritual of key, mortice and bolt. The boy must have barred four doors before he reached the front and said, through the letter-box: 'Who is it, please?'

I could not see the face, but by the voice I would have said the boy was about 13 years old – more of a tikno than a chavi. I introduced myself and told him why I was calling, careful not to sound like some kind of authority.

'My father's not here,' he said. 'He's gone shopping.' Minstead's one shop I had already visited, and it seemed Dado might be taking his usual roundabout route home.

But nobody in the public bar of the Servant had the Romany look about him. There was Trevor in the trilby, whom I had seen before. He sits under a Karsh-type photographic study of a rustic – a cherrywood pipe-bowl of a face, with a soft trilby crammed down upon it and fine white sideburns pushing from under the brim. Trevor, the image of this image, sits watching you as you look at him, and back at the picture; showing no amusement or surprise.

There was the Major, genial but taciturn, embraced by many of the remarks but content to nod and smile and play the silent partner.

The others could have been Johns, Harrys, Dans, and they switched easily from politics to the headlines and to the latest local scandal which involved a shotgun and a lady's virtue.

And there was Jeremy Roughton, the youngest member, with black, curly hair and a vivacity that was almost Romanichàl in itself, who was to take me on the next stage of my little odyssey.

But first I switched their talk to gypsies. I recalled the confrontation between Coopers and Witchers which had barred the travellers from the Servant and could well have begun in this very bar. They looked blank. I understood, I said, that a new landlord had been brought in as a direct result. But the stocky character behind the bar did not share the recollection. These were certainly not the circumstances of his coming, he said.

He was not offended, however; more intrigued, and in a short space of time I was being informed, right, left and centre.

The wartime inhabitants of Shave Green weren't the proper gypsies, John, were they?

No. There were a lot of deserters. Whenever anybody from the Southampton area went missing from his unit, the police came straight to Shave Green.

No. These weren't the genuine travellers, or they would have been . . . travelling.

Well, perhaps there might have been *some* true Needies . . .

One lesson you learn quickly in conversations with Forest folk is their appetite for the sweeping generalisation. Furthermore, they rarely let the facts get in the way of a good story. That is not a criticism. It is not even a point of social uniqueness. You find dramatic elaboration in any homely community where contact is by word of mouth. It is a game – and the secret of acceptance in these communities is in learning to play it well.

Trevor, for instance, plays it as to the manner born.

Born and raised on a farm at St Hilary, Cowbridge – 12 miles or so from my own Cardiff beginnings – he left there some 50 years ago (though two sisters still remain) and spent his working life leading stallions around Hants, Wilts and Dorset from one covering commission to the next. It sounded like a solitary kind of existence, one at least that could not easily be shared, and for some reason or another, when he finally came to rest in Minstead a few years ago, he was wifeless – and prey to the local wags' pointed inquiries about his ability to cope.

He had his own kind of serialised responses which have grown over the years to mythical proportions.

Some of the alleged turns of events are indelicate for a family readership but the most uproarious sections are concerned with his vain efforts to take his 90-year-old housekeeper – there is, of course, no 90-year-old housekeeper – for a slap-up dinner at the New Forest Hotel, Emery Down.

When Trevor entertains, he does it in the grand manner and thus, hot steak and kidney pies had been ordered for 7.30 at the Forest inn.

But when the taxi came to convey the handsome couple to their repast, it was discovered that the lady was too bandy to get both legs into the taxi at the same time. So they reset the date, recounted Trevor, and this time he ordered a Pickford's removal van to make sure of sufficient space and then went ahead to the hotel to confirm their booking.

But two hours later, his companion still hadn't arrived, and on returning home he found the pantechnicon standing there and his housekeeper seated miserably in its confines. He asked the driver about the delay.

'Sorry,' said the driver. 'Rules of the firm. I can't go without a full load.'

The story goes on and on, swelled nightly (and mid-daily) by the latest inspiration to come from Trevor's habitual Guinness, and the locals love it and love him for it.

But Trevor himself, it seemed, gained almost as much enjoyment from my own *faux pas* with the photograph on the wall.

When you study the features side by side with more than casual intensity, the separate identities are clear. The man on the wall is Jack Storms, one-time gamekeeper to the Comptons at Minstead Manor, and the people who recall him are getting rarer and rarer. For all that, he and Trevor had certain common factors.

One man who knew Jack Storms was C.R. Acton ('Sydney the Standard' of *Horse and Hound*), who features the old keeper in a cameo in his *Sport and Sportsmen of the New Forest* (1936).

Nearly 50 years ago, Jack Storms was already an old man and Acton wrote of '. . . a wonderful character. A weather-worn bowler hat at a rakish angle surmounts a yet more weatherworn, wrinkled visage, clean-shaven and fringed with white whiskers. Usually, he carries a most incongruous looking umbrella under his arm but, however wet the day, I have never seen him hold it up! What Jack doesn't know about the animal life of Minstead and its surroundings is not worth picking up.

'Jack knows the whereabouts of a badger close at hand and the old man – no one has the slightest idea of Jack's age, like the Forest oaks that he so much resembles, he seems eternal – shows us the little path that Brock has trodden into the thick rhododendrons . . .'

The badger caught and the evening coming down softly, the ageless keeper has another lesson to deliver. 'Here, old Jack gives us a further education – it is on how to lower a quart of beer out of a bottle, non-stop! Verily, a man of parts is the old Minstead keeper.'

But how did anyone persuade Jack Storms to be photographed? He seems the sort who would share gypsy matriarch Priscilla Wells's contempt and suspicion for anything mechanical. Priscilla would have looked upon the box camera as a coffin and its shutter as a blind dropped upon her life.

'Photographer chap came down from London for the weekend – high society type,' said Trevor. 'Had a nice bit of stuff with him. Jack was probably looking at her.'

You could almost believe him.

Jeremy Roughton, meanwhile, had promised me sight of pictures taken at a gypsy wedding just before Shave Green ceased to be a compound – pictures and a chat with his mother, Iseult, who could – if anybody could – tell me how things had really been at Shave Green. On his moped, Jeremy led my car back over the dipping lanes, streaming now with the downpour that had been on the cards all morning, and turned me in over the cattle grid at an entrance which had been intriguing me since I had seen it earlier: 'To Suters Cottage Only'.

The farm was a settlement in the middle of a clearing in Shave Wood. In some form or another, it had probably been there for centuries, but the red-brick was a fairly recent manifestation – only a century or so old. Ponies grazed on the surrounding lawn, and at other times, one suspected, they might well give way to deer; for here, indeed, was the heart of the Forest, a dwelling so integral and so close to enchantment that one half expected it to be made of gingerbread.

And the most marked evidence of its authenticity was the most recent and ultra-modern innovation – a relic of a recent episode from the BBC's science-fiction series, *Blake's Seven.* It was a mantrap – a thoroughly convincing construction of spiked branches which a technician portraying the far-out future had created in reproducing the primitive past. It was a nice irony that gave further point to my case of timelessness once the branches close overhead.

Mrs Roughton and her family were almost newcomers to the farm, tenants of the Forestry Commission. Prior to this placing, they had operated the horse-drawn carts which one sees all too infrequently, for some reason, upon Forest roads. And Mrs Roughton's love for such a mode is hardly diminished. She is a prime mover – and that really is the phrase – with the New Forest section of the British Driving Society.

This contact keeps her in touch with the Establishment and they with her. It is just one of a complex structure of friendships and acquaintances which make up the environment of the true Forester – where artisan rubs shoulders with aristocrat, Commissioner with Commoner, journalist (hopefully) with gypsy. It isn't possible to keep a foot in all camps because nobody has that many feet. But they try, those decapod dreamers, how they try . . .

While Mrs Roughton regaled me with recollections of the days at Burley Rails, her sister in Cornwall, her first meeting in that far corner with Sven Berlin 30 years ago – 'The women used to flock around him like flies; I don't know why' – Jeremy dug out the albums and newspaper cuttings and then made some tea. Mugs of handsome proportions for himself and me, a delicate flowered cup and saucer that looked like Crown Derby for his mother.

The wedding had been conducted by Pete Ingram – 'Gypsy Pete', Jeremy called him. 'I don't know if he actually is of the blood royal, but he likes to think so.'

Pete, now settled with his wife, artist Juliet Jeffery, in Selborne, had painted the little dog-cart which stood outside Suters Cottage. Flowers and horses, a three-day job carried out for the well-loved lady he and Juliet call 'Aunty Wizzy'.

Pete, it was accepted in the compound, had the power to join people, and the young couple who mingled blood and jumped the bonfire at Shave Green – our picture is by Burley photographer Simon Rowley, who gained what the Press call an 'exclusive' of the event – were employees of the Gypsy Lore Society who had been teaching the local chavis for some months. The commitment was binding, in the eyes of the Romanies, but the couple later went through a more widely recognised ceremony at a properly authorised place.

Juliet first became aware of the gypsies from the caravans which passed by her Sussex village when she was a child. In her adult years, she followed the caravans to their famous fair at Appleby, Westmorland, and took along

Gypsy wedding. Pete Ingram marries two young social workers and, following tradition, they jump the bonfire (*opposite*).

her sketch book. A result was a most picturesque teaming of Jeffery drawings and the poetry of 'Lavengro' (a name not Borrowed from George but a genuine Romany term, 'Man of words'): *The Gypsy* (Midas Books, 1973).

Peter and Juliet, at their Romany museum in the village more usually associated with Gilbert White, might have provided a palpable link, but they were on the edge of the wrong forest – Wolmer. Although I would hold a meeting with them as a treat for some time in the future, my immediate trail needed a new direction.

Perhaps that could be found at Thorney Hill, site of another compound. But for the moment, in this north-east shoulder of the woods, I had another call to make.

Priscilla Wells, mother of Jesse, had been Queen of Shave Green in a black felt hat with a large violet bow, a tattered Victorian armchair for a

throne, a Stuart nose as proof of her link with royalty (Frances and Winifred Wells are the names linked with Charles II in the Brockenhurst area) and a jackdaw as her court jester. Sven Berlin, setting out to sketch her, had this to say: 'Like a duck, Pris Wells did not seem to know where her person left off and the landscape began. The jackdaw was part of her foot; when it flew on to her hat, it was part of her head, and when it flew to a tree her foot or head was part of the tree . . .

'While I was painting Pris I saw Dosha pass through her and Benny and Jesse. She became a multiple person from whom her loved ones were not divided by space or flesh. I saw also a King of England, an Eastern princess, and I saw an ancient Goddess of an Invaded Moon. I called her Luna . . .'

Jesse at his going had filled Minstead and surrounds with gypsies. Luna, at her parting, held up the traffic for miles on the main road from London, Winchester, Romsey into the Forest.

Travelling that road, the cortege came to a standstill and the coffin was lifted out of the hearse and set upon trestles. Then the lid was unscrewed and removed, and in the gentle drizzle the gypsy mourners began their procession. While the young girls and women decorated the body, the face, the silk interior, the shroud with small roses and fern, the others filed past, each brushing the features, cold as stone, with their lips. Wailing women had to be lifted aside while the lid was restored and the Queen moved on to Copythorne Cemetery.

If rain is a matter of perpetual cyclic motion between earth, sea and air, it is possible that a little of that same drizzle moistened my own shoulders as I stood here in Copythorne more than 20 years on.

Such a massive wake these days would not have the same paralytic effect upon the traffic because the M27 rips and roars alongside that old Romsey road like a tidal river paralleling a spring. By that same token, no similar entourage of mourners could gather on the surrounding slopes between this uphill graveyard and Newbridge, Fursley, Nomansland – the grim reaper from the Department of the Environment has cut a yellow-grey swathe through the countryside and the opportunities as well as the trees have fallen. There is a limit now to the number of people who can get close enough to be touched by an occasion.

If Jesse's resting place is unidentifiable, that of his mother (and now his brother, Benny) is unmistakable. Minstead churchyard may turn its gypsy inhabitants into enigmas but to the right of the gate, at Copythorne's lowest point, the cemetery spells out its Coopers, its Witchers, its Greens. And the grave of Priscilla Wells has this to say: 'How we miss her, aching hearts alone can tell. We have lost her, Heaven has found her. Jesu has done all things well . . . From her sorrowing sons and daughter.'

Of the sorrowing children, only Benny joined her and earned the formality of 'Benjamin' on the opposite side the rectangular sepulchre from his mother's legend and dedication.

While cancer ravaged his throat and a stroke immobilised him, sister Harriet kept him supplied with the Polo mints which, too late, had replaced the habitual cigarettes. But one day she developed a brain tumour and the next day, she was dead. The following day, Benny himself was no more. In the same week that Harriet was cremated, Benny came to the hill.

The grave is grand in Romany terms but simple among those who honour death with extravagance. There is no doubting, however, which one gets the brighter and more regular flowers. The grandchildren remember – wherever they are.

They are not at Thorney Hill.

The area where the local council erected prefabricated chalets to house the travellers, thinking that that might have been an improvement on their canvas or wheeled concoctions, was semi-cleared for a long time, with brambles thriving upon the concrete standings. Now, even the concrete is gone to make a car-free zone and the lawn is so authentic – the product of an alliance between the Forestry Commission and New Forest District Council – that it might always have been that way.

Down the road towards Bransgore, several council houses have a slightly wild look about them, as though their tenants would sooner be out than in. But these same people have already announced to the local authority that they are not Needies or Diddekoi or tinker or anything in between. They are householders, just like the rent book says. If you were looking for roots, they would lean over the chain-link fences which separate their gardens from the road and deny them.

Brian Vesey-Fitzgerald dates the deterioration of the gypsy tradition from 1926, when an Act of Parliament forced the travellers into ordered communities and really believed it was removing blots from landscapes.

But some time earlier, Elizabeth Godfrey cited 'the Missioner, the Board School and the perpetual harass of having to move on.' She added: 'If the Board School system is turning out a failure for our little peasants, what can we say for it when it claims the gypsy? The gypsy child cannot assimilate book-learning. He goes in sharp as a needle, cunning as a fox, sagacious with ancient woodland lore, long-sighted, keen of ear and scent; he comes out stupid, blear-eyed, often slightly deaf. The new knowledge drops away from him in a month; the old has been stamped out. You have made of him a lazy good-for-nothing, liable to colds and ailments hitherto unknown.'

An old wives' tale had it that the gypsies stole children. I wonder whether the truth of it was that the children stole the gypsies.

It is generally believed that there was spontaneous outcry against gypsies by residents of the Forest. But in all his dealings with the true Foresters over a period of more than 50 years, Vesey-Fitzgerald never found any deep-seated hostility. The trouble began, he reasoned, in the years after World War I when the 'newly-wealthy townsfolk, jealous of their status,' began moving in and worrying about 'the tone of the place'.

The New Forest Committee, 1947, in their White Paper, claimed: 'While the standard of people throughout the country is steadily being raised, a group is allowed to live in the Forest which has hardly reached the standard of the Stone Age. The gypsies, it is true, have not been heard in their own defence, but we have visited their camps and we should hesitate to describe them in detail.

'Even the picturesque element which appeals to the imagination of their defenders is here entirely lacking. Whatever may have been the case in earlier times, those of today show little of the true Romany strain and a very few only maintain the old Romany way of life with its comparatively high standards.'

Here, then, spoke the Voice of Authority and since these conservative newcomers were on the Side of Authority, there seemed little argument, particularly since the gypsies themselves were not sufficiently gifted in tongues to make much headway against the patter of protocol.

The year 1926 could have marked the beginning of the end and, as an historic milestone, it must be valid. But I see the Fall as far more gradual and as traditional as the peacock and its exit from Julia Berlin's bedhead Eden. The gypsies were marked for death from the day of their birth.

Now? Perhaps only those with the special affinity, the third eye, can find them. I covered miles to no avail, found places where the deepest evidence of their presence was in the level of nostalgia. But the Needies – the ones who called the New Forest their 'Neva Wesh' – are no longer leaving signs.

In mid-1978, Sven Berlin sent me a charming note. He and Julia, he said, had found Rosie of the family of Wells selling cowslips in Lymington Market. Quite by chance.

I thought of hot-footing it to Lymington to seek out the vivacious features which Berlin wanted so much to get on canvas. But then I thought again. On my day, Rosie of the house of Wells would not be there. Not for me.

One odd little incident came out of my visit to Minstead. Jeremy Roughton had told me a story about a friend who had a horse – surprising how many Forest stories begin just so – and this horse would not go near Bignell Wood, one-time home of Sir Arthur Conan Doyle. The house, it seemed, was haunted. There were good, honest, sober, hard-working people who had passed there by moonlight and seen the ghost of the old gentleman sitting in a tree, reading a book.

This friend, insisted Jeremy, had even been able to smell the paraffin because Doyle, it seemed, had lost his mind before the end and tried to set fire to the place. You could still smell it now.

And the present owner – a Dr McAll – he had invented the Apollo space capsule, said the bar experts at the Green Dragon, which is just down the road from the rambling old house. Altogether the affair was too pregnant with possibilities to be left like that.

As I swung into the shingle drive, a board greeted me, a board which said, as near as makes no matter: 'Drs K. and F. McAll – By Appointment Only'. Well, I had no appointment because it was a sudden whim whose seduction had been growing all the while I tried to give my attention to the gypsies. But here I was, armed with the kind of questions I could not ask without being facetious, anyway – so I took a chance.

I was greeted with utter and captivating charm. The garden, first of all – a cross between a park and a dell, wonderfully endowed with laurel, azalea and daffodil, on either side of a serpentine stretch of the Cadnam River. A water wheel – still under construction by Dr Kenneth, I discovered – and a wooden, covered bridge between house and drive.

The impression was Oriental and exactly right for the residents.

Drs Kenneth and Frances McAll were medical missionaries in China for nearly 20 years, including wartime. Although there were occasions when their European origins could have landed them in trouble – and did as the Japanese moved in – they have a firm and abiding love for the East, and their carpets, their furniture, their ornamentation bespeak the fact.

Dr Frances was at home when I made my unscheduled call – just about, she said ruefully, to watch the Cup Final. Not that she was fond of football, just for something to do. Certainly, a conversation would be much nicer.

A tall lady, bespectacled, fiftyish, with kindly eyes which could always find some comfort for the distressed, East or West. Not so much of a doctor herself now but a helper for her husband and for patients who stayed as guests, now and then.

When I mentioned Conan Doyle and his tree seat and his moonlight reading, she laughed.

'Well, that I hadn't heard – and we know most of the tales because Brigadier John Doyle (nephew of the author, who lives at Whitley Ridge, near Brockenhurst) has become a firm friend of ours and a regular visitor. He did tell us, though, that he and the Doyle children used to dance on a flat roof here at night, just to throw a scare into the colony of gypsies who used to live next door.'

Out of such pranks, legends are born.

And the fire? I had sniffed the air most conscientiously as I made my slow way up to the house and had caught no more than the scents of a spring garden and a running river.

More laughter. 'There might have been a small outbreak when the Doyles had left and the house was empty – but the family certainly never put a match to it.'

A bit of own back, perhaps, from the terrorised neighbours. I laughed myself, recalling the Green Dragon observations and the local love of a good tale. 'Then what,' I said, 'about Apollo?'

'That's true. At least . . . almost true. We were in Texas in 1961 and a friend took us to Houston to look around the National Aeronautics and Space Administration.

'One item we were shown was the interior of the Apollo . . . command module? Is that what it was called? They knew we were medical people with an interest in psychiatry and they asked our opinions on the model, bearing in mind that men were going to have to live for some time in this confined space. They hadn't included any windows because they thought if the astronauts had to look out on the immensity of space, it might be a tax on their nerves.

'My husband – or it might even have been myself – anyway, we both felt that giving the men a view of some sort was vitally important to their orientation. We had had a little taste of confinement with the Japanese, you see, and we knew just how oppressive and – unhinging – unrelieved bare walls could be. We must have sounded quite convincing because, the next thing we knew, they were making a note to include port-holes.

'I remember they were a little bothered, too, about the wheels of the moon buggy. What would happen if the buggy had a puncture? My husband's not an expert, but he does have a mechanical turn of mind and he put a point which he thought was obvious. Why not use solid tyres, he said. And when we were watching the moon landings on television, it really looked as though they had taken him up on it. But it's wrong to say we worked for NASA. We were just given a tour.'

Mission Control, Houston, seemed a long way from Bignell Wood, whose only link with space was the 'docking corridor' of glass which joins what might originally have been two lodges, now used as a conservatory.

Of all the tales woven in ignorance and mischief about this atmospheric dwelling, the latest was perhaps the most incredible. You could believe in ghosts, even arson – but moon buggies? Here?

It's the kind of find that keeps you digging.

A Matter of Distance

IN the Forest it is as well to know your left hand from your right, but this has ceased to be a matter of life and death. Some ageing guidebooks warn soberly that you should not take a step without a compass and a knapsack full of food.

It would be a pity if such formidable advice should tie you to the well-beaten track for all time. Let us just say this – a compass takes up little enough room and a bar of chocolate or a packet of biscuits can be a comfort at times, even if you know exactly where you are. Though please don't leave your wrappers behind; there's precious little protein in Polythene.

I used to think I had a pretty good sense of direction but some matters continually evade me – for instance, you should see me whirling like a Dervish around the Cadnam roundabout, trying to find the road that will take me to the Sir John Barleycorn inn. Modesty forbids me from revealing exactly how many times I have been lost – let us make it Scriptural and say 'a time and times and half a time' – but in fairness to myself and a sidereal instinct which proves more often than not to be positively migratory, I should point that the jammer is not *direction* but *distance*. Time flies, they say, when you are having fun, and the same must be true of feet if they pace out your definition of enjoyment.

Broomy Walk lies between the Linwood-Stoney Cross B road and the A31/M27. Motoring between Cadnam and Picket Post, you will see it to the north as one of the exquisite bands of mixed woodland which share the undulations with raw plain until the whole land takes a final tidal swell and creams up into the Wiltshire Downs. But coming at it from the secondary road, you have no sight or sound of the brash and busy carriageway that underlines it to the south and in so doing emphasises the fact that vandalism is not exclusive to the lawless.

Anyway, coming, as I say, from the north, you turn from a narrow ribbon of grey road into a car park made private by dwarf oaks and gorse and there shed your wheels.

A five-bar gate provides the 'official' access for horses and F.C. vehicles and a kissing-gate alongside lets our heroes in and out. Then a broad ride leads you downhill between varied styles and generations of conifer. Official records put the date of inclosure here at 1809, but perhaps that particular statistic would mean more to the oaks and beeches that maintain a solid if shielded status among these other, younger columns.

On this visit, we turned to the right and followed the track around in a left hand curve towards Amberslade Bottom and then away from it, intending to circle the inclosure without actually leaving the shelter of the trees. The ground was dry but heavily pitted with hoofprints and I recalled Donn Small's words on schools and riders (which you will find in the next chapter).

From time to time, the Nature Conservancy make pronouncements about soil deterioration in the Forest, and here, though conditions could hardly be said to generate alarm – whenever any official body mentions 'deterioration' I have a vision of the Forest slipping away down some massive slope – there was at least a chance to see what the Conservancy meant by the phrase.

The ground was arch and villainous in a manner that bespoke the need for putting sense before style in footwear; but we were shod with sense. The sun was warm, the titmice were garrulous and the butterflies went up like parachutists in reverse from the path ahead of us.

Just as all cats are grey in the dark and all birds are brown on the wing, so all butterflies are white in the sun – specks of bright dust or flashes of white light – which is a shame in a small way because the local lepidoptera vocabulary is considerable. That fragment of sunshine jigging away from you down the ride could be no more than a cabbage white. But suppose it were a clouded yellow or a crimson spotted footman, Purple Emperor, Sponsa, Promissa, Nupta, Valezina, Paphia, rare turn of Sybilla? All might be weighed in the balance of probabilities.

Then before I could confess that I wouldn't know a moth from a Meliloti came evidence of deer.

If all the ferns in Broomy were laid end to end, they would establish some kind of record, for sure. But of course, ferns don't lie, they stand. And they wave at times for no apparent reason, a single leaf seemingly troubled by its own individual breeze.

Scan fern expanses for ripples and you will soon appreciate how complete a cover they provide. Short in the stem though these specimens were, they could have given a hide to a reclining animal and even a ceiling to the activities of the muntjac, the smallest of the Forest deer, already noted at Mark Ash, which was not an impossible distance from here.

There had been a bullet-shaped dropping, a slight doggy smell, nothing conclusive. But now, overshadowing us, was a proof harsh as well as final. A culling tower.

Picture the design from those prisoner-of-war films – four legs with cross-pieces lashed and nailed, a rough ladder up one side and at the top, a platform for spotlight, binoculars or gun. I wondered at first how the deer could possibly miss it – but in a world of upright beams, four more make little impact. It is the movement that alerts deer, not the standing still.

Not the *sitting* still. Former Deputy Surveyor Arthur Cadman begins his book, *Dawn, Dusk and Deer*, from just such a perch, and although it isn't possible to pinpoint it, certainly this part of the Forest was among his favourite places.

But on this warm afternoon out of the season of death, fond recollections were far from my thoughts. One tower led us to another and another and it was a while before we could put aside the sinister purpose and let our own curiosity guide us up the steps to get our heads among the branches.

If deer have a folklore or mythology, there must be some mention of Broomy, this place where thunder comes in a clear dawn and strikes down so many of their number. While we had been hoping for some sign or sight of them, now we wished the opposite, with the creatures miles distant and their lesson learned.

Our circular tour took us through new woodland and old, with oak and silver birch dominating the lower reaches of this inclosure and spruce succeeding to the rest. We must have walked for about two hours until we came upon a ride that looked like our original and led up to a five-bar gate. But when we emerged from the plantation, the car park was gone.

Far along the road to our left, a clump of growth seemed familiar and we began our trek towards it, finding peat-black paths among the cushions of heather. The clump was a car park, all right – but not ours. This was Spring Bushes and, in my faulty knowledge of that time, we must have been too circular in our route.

I took thought. Broomy, I reasoned, must be towards Stoney Cross, and I began moving with haste in that direction, covering a good half-mile before I would admit that I might be wrong. The complete absence of anything resembling a car park, let alone a car that we knew, made a denial useless anyway.

My wife had been pointing the expert towards Linwood from the beginning but the expert had been too busy being the expert to take any notice. Now we trudged back in the direction she had indicated with the gap between myself and my charges growing all the time – hysterical laughter does tend to slow you down.

It was on a visit to Cadnam that we met Brian Hayward and his charming wife. Brian is a thatcher and has problems his forefathers never knew; not because the art of thatching is in decline, but because it is thriving. Brian's ancestors, working out of the Fordingbridge area for the last 500 years, could be sure of what they were doing, and once they knew their bale straw from their Norfolk reed each commission became a simple matter of application. But these days, more often than not, Brian finds himself playing the carpenter before he can lay a strand.

Brian and Sandra were giving a new crown to the Sir John Barleycorn; a three-month task and straightforward, Sir John having been barley-topped from the beginning. 'The trouble comes,' said Brian, 'when people want to introduce thatch on to roofs that were designed for tiles. The system of joists is all different and often they have to be replaced. But apart from that there are so many nooks and crannies to get into.'

Brian hasn't found any roof that has beaten him yet, but he is picking up a whole new box of tricks as he goes and it is likely to come in handy when his younger brother leaves school and, without question, enters the family business, and when the next wave of Haywards breaks on Fordingbridge and comes combing out across the Forest.

For all the rigours of what is rapidly turning into a new science, Brian has help, too, that his forebears never had – a wife who doesn't mind donning a pair of jeans and following him up the ladder to pass the golden stems to him as he plaits and kneads and persuades.

Nervous? 'To begin with,' admitted Sandra. 'But you get used to it. It takes me out of the house – and I enjoy meeting people.'

We left the Haywards to their lunch of sandwiches, cake and canned mineral water, and we will run across them again, for sure, because there are so many thatches in the Forest area and Hayward is such a mighty name after five centuries.

And they started us looking at those roof-tops with rather more than the

Thatches at Swan Green – probably the best-known in the Forest area.

usual 'that's-pretty' interest.

Perhaps the best-known thatch work is on the terraced row of cottages which overlooks the cricket field at Swan Green, on the outskirts of Lyndhurst, and beautiful and clean and solid as it is, it is not the finest example available of the thatcher's art.

At Furzey Gardens, on the hill above Minstead, a museum and standing craft exhibition will give you a better idea of the variations but even that cannot compare with the little cottage that looms up out of nowhere along a country lane and takes your breath away.

Along the A338 – not if you are driving because the road seems to draw more than its fair share of fools and you need all your concentration – at Ibsley, there are three or four absolute showpieces, not least the Old Beams pub and restaurant.

One of our particular favourites is not in the Forest proper but at the bypass end of the B3081 Ringwood-Verwood road, looking as if it has been lifted bodily from those wonderful fairy-tale illustrations that splashed colour on our childhood.

There is another on the dipping, twisting little road that takes you from Burley to the A35 via Lucy Hill, South Oakley and Anderwood inclosures.

Two more of the older variety look up to the Green Dragon at Brook and the byways around Minstead, Newtown and Emery Down and in the

An old thatch near Canterton – some of the most picturesque roofs are hidden up country lanes.

Bramshaw, Canterton, Fritham area are dotted with such delights.

It is a book in itself, this thatching, like so many of the Forest specialities – and so many of the characters who generated those specialities over the years.

The compulsive way of the Forest is how it keeps you coming back to learn more not only about places but about people – people like Gerald and Hubert Forward, agister brothers who have served the Swainmote (Gerald as a Verderer, too) for half a century; Elizabeth Short, daughter of painter Golden Short and the photographer whose work is celebrated in so many of those recently-printed postcards of the old Forest, thanks to the work of her granddaughter, Mrs K. Selfe, of Bolton's Bench; Brusher Mills – if you have heard of only one local character, the chances are that it was Brusher; Mr Maldwin Drummond and his cousin, Belinda, former Lady Montagu, the powers behind a tapestry produced by the New Forest Association to mark the Forest's 900th year; whose dedication to Forest matters, committees and interests leaves them little time for anything else – not that they want anything else; the late Sir Colin Ziegler, whose contribution to the Forest may well be memorialised shortly by a bridge or some other amenity in one of his favourite spots; his daughter, Mrs Lesley Errington, a hard-working member of New Forest District Council; Miss Dionis McNair, a Verderer and a friend to every pony; and a dozen, a hundred, a thousand quiet folk who all find their own peace in providing it for the rest of us.

All of these are worth more than a passing mention, but their commitment to their endeavours rations the time they have available for interviewers. Let it nevertheless be stated that the New Forest would be a far lesser place but for their timely presence.

Peace or Pipelines?

TODAY there are two concrete threats to the Forest, one social and one technological – and hopefully it will be the imminence of the latter that will resolve the former. Without such a settlement another Doomsday could be very close indeed . . . and a Doomsday very different from the reckoning which began our account.

The social problem first. In a nutshell, it might be described as an excess of partisanship.

Like other matters which have more than one side, the environmental commitment depends largely upon where you stand – so that one lobby may rage at too many conifers while another, with equal dedication, may contend that their removal is a danger to the honey buzzard.

For instance . . . A fairly constant agitation from the Commoners is for the drainage of valley bogs. The waterlogged areas are growing, they claim, and as a consequence the zones for grazing are subject to shrinkage. The conservationist's answer to that is – if you dry out the bogs, you will lose molinia (purple moor grass) which happens to be a staple food for the grazers.

The Commoner's reply to the conservationist is that he doesn't mind losing a bit of molinia if he can save a few ponies from drowning, and he suggests that the conservationist would like to have all cattle and ponies out of the Forest to keep it for birds, butterflies and bog orchids.

At this point, relations tend to become rather chilly. The dispute is hardly diminished by the fact that certain memories – perhaps the faulty ones, perhaps the not-so-faulty – recall that this particular stretch presents nothing like the hazard that was there in grandfather's day. And the confusion is certainly increased by the fact that such nostalgia doesn't seem to favour any one side.

The Nature Conservancy would like to see the open Forest worked on a rotation basis, with large areas ploughed up in turn to aerate the earth and ease the problem of worm infestation, which reaches its peak on such areas as Stoney Cross airfield, flat, forgotten and grazed to the quick.

The Forest could be divided into three regions easily enough, Colin Tubbs of the Nature Conservancy has worked out, with the closure of underpasses. What is needed, he says, is proper range management – but nobody will grasp the nettle, let alone come up with the money. The Commoners won't wear the wholesale removal of facilities, even for a short term – and with the redworm laying something like 100,000 eggs at a sitting, ploughshares, they say, will make hardly any difference, except to bounce the little beggars around a bit.

The dense growth of furze in some places has led certain experts to suggest that the ponies are changing their feeding habits. At time of writing, two Southampton University students are preparing a treatise, sponsored by the Nature Conservancy, on just this subject. The Commoners, whose good will rather than any inherent funds can just about run to an annual sponsored ragwort pull, do not need a treatise to provide their answer. The plain fact is, they say, that the gorse is 25 years old and more, over the top in stature and nourishment.

This is precisely the kind of scrub which is at the thorny centre of the 'burning question'. Each year between January 1 and March 31, the Forestry Commission carries out controlled burning, ashes being the best way to encourage fresh growth of ferns and bracken.

The size of areas to be so scorched is a matter for tight-lipped negotiation between Commission and Commoners, with the Court of Verderers then adding the necessary approval. For January-March, 1978, the agreed figure was 1,000 acres. Because of the damp winter, the Commission could only clear between 300 and 400 acres, even by extending the burning season to April 15. The embargo is at Nature Conservancy insistence, because from late March or mid-April on, the wildlife is regenerating.

The Commoners do not hate wildlife and their usual argument is with conservator, not conserved. The fauna, they feel, do not need the spoon-feeding which the naturalists claim is so essential.

The Commission's failure to reach its target – not for the first time – is seen by the Commoners as a deliberate device to renege on promises. Back comes the answer from the Conservancy that if the Commoners would only clear the dead bracken which litters the heaths, they could create conditions to produce new browsing matter, and burning would no longer be so necessary.

The Commoners, says Mrs Pam Harvey Richards, who is by way of being a spokesperson though an unofficial one (her bars at Brook are decorated with leather plaques showing 300 of the local brands and there are around a thousand more besides) are probably the one agency that has changed least in 900 years. And in nine centuries, it has to be conceded, the run of play has very seldom been in their favour.

If they look askance now at a proposition which may seem perfectly reasonable in contemporary terms, it is because they see the thing in the panoramic context. In the past, the most apparently innocent innovation has too often left them with land worth or measuring that much less.

It is this trustless situation which leads Colin Tubbs, watching the situation not just from his comfortable cabin in the Queen's House car park but also from the grass-roots level, to believe that the main problem in the next few years will come from inside and not outside the Forest – a direct confrontation between Commoners and Conservancy over the way each of them runs his particular aspect of the operation.

But there cannot be agreement even on that. Verderer Anthony Pasmore, who has a large number of dealings with the Commoners and whose family enjoys good standing with the smallholders, laughs off the idea of such a face-to-face. 'Such a war would be no war at all,' he says. 'The Conservancy would wipe the floor with the Commoners. It has all the power of a major Governmental office and a national machinery to create sympathy for its cause. The Commoners have a little pull locally but not much – and their ability to communicate a sympathetic image of their own is sadly limited by lack of funds and lack of expertise. They would go to the wall – and most outsiders would believe that was justice.'

Mr Pasmore's listing of major hazards is rather more formal, but even so it does not find complete agreement with the Deputy Surveyor, Mr Donn Small. Mr Pasmore still puts mass invasion at the head of his list.

Since his installation, Mr Small has moved heaven and earth – or, at least, common and conifer – to ensure that the public amenity shall not become the private hell. He has surrounded car parks and caravan sites with 'dragon's teeth' and saved valuable woodland from anything heavier than feet, as well as providing an information service for everybody whose interest is more than peripheral. Thus, he contends, he has given recreation the attention it deserves; no more and no less. He is confident that the careful projections made over the last eight to ten years and the measures taken to meet them have produced facilities well able to cope with a people boom significantly larger than any manifested to date.

Monitoring taken at various caravan sites in the last couple of years on public holidays would seem to indicate that a peak has been reached and contained, he says. But the actual figures make his assurances sound slightly optimistic. Worked out in 'camper nights' (that is, one person camping for one night), the outstanding statistics show that in the long, hot summer of 1976, for instance, there were ten times as many campers (838,000) as there had been in 1956 (83,000). But those details have less impact with me than some of the others which, in general, indicate an upward trend annually of anything between 9,000 and 40,000, as well as occasional falls not always explained by bad weather.

Between 1967 and 1968, camper nights rose from 277,000 to 454,000 and subsequent figures have shown that a rise of 100,000 or more in 12 months

People, given proper facilities, are a controllable hazard.

has not been unusual since. The 1969 figure of 520,000 preceded a statistic of 618,500 in 1970. A total of 670,500 in 1973 gave way to 797,700 in 1974.

The peak figure (so far) of 838,000 in 1976 might have been considered an unusual consequence of an unusual year, except that in the indifferent summer of 1977, a total of 811,700 camper nights was recorded – and the 1978 numbers look like telling much the same story.

So we can now quite reasonably consider 800,000-plus as the norm, with a charted tendency for figures to jump by 100,000-to-170,000 in 12 months. In the light of that, it is no great flight of fancy to visualise more than a million camper nights in the very near future . . . and more than two million, on present rate of increase, by the year 2000.

In his *Hampshire Days*, written in 1903 mostly while he was a guest at Royden House, Boldre, W.H. Hudson observed:

'The Forest has been known and loved by a limited number of persons always; the general public have only discovered it in recent years. For one visitor twenty years ago there are scores, probably hundreds today. And year by year, as motoring becomes more common, and as cycling from being general grows, as it will, to be universal, the flow of visitors to the Forest will go on at an ever-increasing rate, and the hundreds of today will be thousands in five years' time . . .

'And as it grows in favour in all the country as a place of recreation and refreshment, the subject of its condition and management, and the ways of its inhabitants, will receive an increased attention. The desire will grow that it shall not be spoilt, either by the authorities or the residents, that it shall not be turned into townships and plantations, nor be starved, nor its wild life left to be taken and destroyed by anyone and everyone . . .'

That must be the last time anybody actually believed the peripatetic hordes were going to do the Forest some good. Not even the Royal Society for the Protection of Birds, who owe their very foundation to Hudson, would be likely to agree with his sentiments in the light of subsequent developments – and where all those bicycles went, goodness knows.

More and more people in the Forest means deeper and deeper probing for privacy, feels Colin Tubbs, so that the incursions of the determined few will become the excursions of the hounded many, given time.

My own view, based on observations at car parks and cleared areas all over the Forest is more hopeful; in a large number of cases, the 'great rural renaissance' which makes Colin so anxious still goes only as far as flying your kite or emptying your dog.

In 1975–76, Dr Susan Mayne of the Nature Conservancy Council, at the invitation of the Forestry Commission, carried out a survey of Forest areas in regular use by riding establishments. She found that tracks ran to a total length of 227 miles which made up an area of 354 acres. Of that area of vegetation, approximately 70 acres – or 20 per cent – was eroded.

A comparison with aerial photographs taken in 1967 showed that most of the paths existed then in an embryonic stage. The disturbing factor was that in ten years, the tracks had not grown longer, but wider. While 18.7 per cent of them were still less than two metres wide, 67 per cent were between two and six metres across, and the remaining 14 per cent were broader than that – six metres plus, or more than 20 feet in good old British measure.

The matter becomes important because of the difficulty in remedying this wear and tear, particularly where the subsoil has been exposed – a condition which existed at some point along 57 per cent of the paths examined.

Dr Mayne, in her report, made the point: 'The total area of eroded ground at present is relatively small in relation to the Open Forest as a whole, but represents the early stages of a process difficult to reverse.

'The multiplicity of paths "paralleling" is a major visual detraction especially on rising ground, and is fragmenting the heathland in the same way that vehicles were causing damage prior to their exclusion from the car-free areas.'

Spots where these equestrian activities were most marked were deemed high pressure zones, and in mid-1978 four options had been outlined by the Forestry Commission for consideration by the riding establishments.

They are:

i. Designate riding routes to which all riders must adhere and an acceptance of the deterioration of those surfaces.

ii. Designate riding routes in high pressure zones and prepare special soft surfaces to support constant ridings. (Such a surface, of gravel and sand, was laid on the north-east boundary of Brockenhurst to test its performance under regular heavy use. Users have reported that it is satisfactory.)

iii. Retain the freedom of horse riders to choose any route but vary their use according to the weather and management requirements.

iv. Retain freedom of choice of route but close all degraded routes which are scenically unacceptable and create new diversions with specially prepared surfaces.

In March 1978 – the details were released in May 1978 – the New Forest Technical Review Group which comprises Commission, Conservancy, Hampshire County Council, New Forest District Council and representatives of other interested parties under the headship of Official Verderer Sir Dudley Forwood set out its statement of future strategy.

Its proposal on riding and pony trekking was that – while recognising that there was no way of limiting the number of horses in the Forest and that the established rights of the Commoners should be excluded from any provision – the number of riding establishments should be limited to the 35 already in existence, and that serious consideration should be given to controlling this use by licence.

The prospect of licensing had raised its spectral head at least a year earlier and had met with outcries individual and collective from the riding schools. But Donn Small makes this point about any licence fees: 'If we charged each establishment something like £1 a year for each of its horses, that might raise £1,000 a year, probably less. Believe me, that would come nowhere near the kind of money we would be paying out for specially prepared tracks or even for just repairing the degraded areas.'

The Forest pony – as distinct from any mounts working out of the schools – is far too major an agency in Forest ecology to be dismissed as mere fauna. It has been called the architect of the woodland, and more particularly of the Open Waste, but it is so much more – and so much less, by some reckoning, because the little consumer-designer is only as good as the price it fetches.

A Forest without the pony would soon be impenetrable. Climb over a fence on the A35 from grazed to ungrazed pasture – as Anthony Pasmore did – and you see the marked difference. Take a place like Pennington Common,

Ponies, despite the nuisance, are vital to Forest ecology.

which was freed of ponies when the cattle grids went down in the mid-1960s, and you discover nothing short of a jungle, with furze patches up to 30 feet high.

Out of well over 1,000 people with Common rights – some of them live in Boscombe, Bournemouth, and for them, the Forest might be somewhere near the Arctic Circle – only about 300 utilise those rights today. It is a matter of wonder to Anthony Pasmore – who, as a land agent, has a professional as well as a personal interest in prevailing trends – that this depleted number still manage to keep as many ponies on the Forest as browsed there in historic times.

Now and then, a Commoner dies with no issue to follow him and his property goes to a Southampton businessman or someone retiring from farther afield. They like the idea of having Forest rights – it sounds great when you say it in the pub – but certainly have no intention of exercising those rights. In 50 years or even 25, the right, true Commoner could be so rare that a browsing crisis would be imminent.

In that event, says Anthony – and he is certainly not joking – there would be a necessity for a State-owned herd of Forest ponies. Forestry Commission, Min of Ag, Nature Conservancy . . . somebody would have to provide and maintain the nibblers or risk the Forest taking on a quite unaccustomed primeval density.

The alternative would be another precedent – some kind of herbicidal control which has not been required up to this time. Forest streams are remarkable for their clarity and cleanliness by virtue of the farming practised in their catchment areas – dairy, with the grass kept short by entirely natural means. There is no danger of a silent spring in the New Forest area under the present circumstances.

The Forest has little enough to fear from fundamental forces – bar one, whose genesis is not natural by any means . . . FIRE.

During the drought of 1976, the Forest had a remarkable escape while its neighbour, Ringwood Forest, was affected in a major way. Travellers now between Ringwood and Verwood can see on either side devastating evidence of what uncontrolled burning can do. These were conifer nurseries and their destruction has set the Forestry Commission back a quarter of a century or more in that area.

More charred trunks can be seen on the undulating Ringwood/Matchams/Hurn road which dodges along at the side of the spur, now touching, now crossing, now putting a good quarter mile of woodland between them – a spot well blessed with caravan sites.

In the same evergreen woodland at St Leonards, a kennel and its dogs were wiped out, old people had to be evacuated from a hospital as flames licked close and troops and firemen joined forces to keep the blaze from reaching an oil storage depot which, if not exactly a military secret, had certainly not been advertising its presence up to that time.

The one good thing that might be said of the scorching between Ringwood and Verwood was that it did clear the road of the mist which rolled off the Avon in quite manageable evening quantities and then developed pea soup profundity by the time it had filtered through the conifers and on to the road. It gave animals a wrong sense of security and raised in motorists that kind of lemming instinct which seems to attach to good roads and bad visibility.

The New Forest, as I said, missed most of the 1976 disaster – only one per cent of its area was affected and all of that was heathland so that Scots pine, hazel and furze were the only tree casualties.

It was pure good fortune.

On the spot investigations showed that fires started on or near the roadside, which hinted strongly at human participation. Cigarettes, matches, discarded bottles, sparks glanced from stones were all put forward as possible causes.

The call from the local Press, as the blackened areas grew and the sun stayed in the sky, was for closure of the Forest while there was still some of it left. The Commission's reaction – and possibly it was the right one; certainly, it was effective – was to plead with the public to give the Forest a miss in the light of the evidence.

Certainly, there was a marked response during August and the Late Summer Bank Holiday period and the record day visitor figures for that year had been accumulated largely before the usual summer peak had been reached – which only goes to show, really, how close we could have got to the *million* camper nights if there had not been this deterrent.

Whether you call it ignorance or irresponsibility, this tendency of people to carry fire with them and to leave it behind when they go is something which must be considered in the designing of recreation areas and in projections on future usage. The Commission seem to feel it would be less than democratic to do more than suggest. So the walks carry fire warning signs and, at intervals, there are stands of beaters, long poles with rubber flaps, for use in the event, if you like. But the pathology of the forest fire displays a process that is slow and surreptitious. An outbreak can spend hours getting above a smoulder – and by the time it is a fire worthy of the name, extinguishing is too big a job for any amateur.

The passive approach may be the right one while visitor numbers remain below a certain level or while people can be dissuaded before they actually arrive. But *over* that figure and *after* that arrival, the odds of disaster begin to shorten and a stage may be reached where polite notices and beaters will not be equal to the task.

That is fire. Water?

We have seen already that the Forest, by its very nature, can be damp for a large part of the year, but while the water sources remain unchanged the problem will always be one of waterlogging rather than flooding.

It is an environmental reality that removal of trees alters drainage habits dramatically and this is a condition more true of the Forest edges than of the woodland itself.

At Barton-on-Sea and Highcliffe, both villages which have grown tremendously in recent years, the local authority have had to spend thousands of pounds on measures to curtail what looks like a rapid rate of cliff erosion which has eaten into gardens and threatens to undermine seafront houses. Various shoring-up techniques have been tried and just lately, progress seems to have been made. But locals of long standing will tell you that there always have been good times and bad times for cliff falls, even though the four gentle tides a day have been constant. They believe that the trouble comes from inland – and that the clearing of trees to make more housing estates, private and public, is the cause. The adjoining strata of chalk and clay are treacherous, they say. The chalk holds the water and the clay slips on it.

Whether that is an articulation of passion or plate tectonics, nobody has yet seen fit to test. Suffice to say that a ban on building homes here is about as likely as a reduction in local bus fares.

Not, I am sure, to redress the balance of nature but to underline the sanctity of tree preservation orders, local councils do take individuals to court for unauthorised lopping and chopping, and single fines can and do run into hundreds of pounds.

Of the other two elements, the earth has already made its claim – in what grows here and what doesn't, in defining where woodland shall give way to heath and valley bog – and the air has little enough to say. When it moves at speed, there is a ninepin result, but in general currents stay well down the Beaufort scale. A hurricane recorded in the early 1700s may well have been no more than a gale puffed up by an enthusiastic reporter.

No, the nuisance from the air today is volume, not velocity. The main north-east/south-west flightpath for Hurn Airport crosses Rhinefield, Holmsley, Thorney Hill, Sopley. Though the lowest altitudes are at the Hurn end of the line, you still find that, at certain periods in high summer, there is an almost continuous buzz and whine of aircraft passing above you as you seek out solitude in the arboretum.

It is certain there is no hazardous level involved here. Counters would barely measure the passage. Jet exhausts at that height are hardly likely to lacerate the great Hampshire sky and let in those damaging gamma rays.

The traffic could not be criticised as offending any of the established thresholds for tolerance. The irritation is to concentration and not to eardrums.

The last White Paper on U.K. civil aviation prospects left Hurn strictly in the middle reaches of the smaller provincial airport list, with a capacity to accommodate the lesser giants in the event of Heathrow fog. This was much to the chagrin of the Hurn Airport Committee of Bournemouth Council, who would like to see the field gain status and business, but much to the liking of the Hurn Airport Action Group, who would sooner have it not there at all.

The small comfort for the Forest underling was that the buzzing would not be increasing to any great degree.

There is, of course, the risk of an accident on any run into or out of an airport and there are all-too-frequent examples of the havoc a renegade aircraft can wreak among trees. But to dwell too much on that would be to lose sight of the fact that the real tragic loss in those circumstances would be lives and not lumber.

A decade ago, Colin Tubbs, in his *The New Forest: An Ecological History*, was warning against sand and gravel extraction as a major threat. The plateau gravel sources on the western fringe of the Forest had been subjected to a number of excavations, he stated, and the annual local demand – about 520,000 cubic yards, as estimated in the Report of the Advisory Committee on Sand and Gravel, 1950 – had risen to at least double that figure, on average, between 1959 and 1963.

'Already,' he said in 1968, 'some limited exploitation of the gravels on some of the manorial wastes within the Forest has taken place or is in progress, and further extraction is contemplated.'

Previously, he had warned: 'Excavation often involves the barbaric mutilation of open heathland scenery, which inevitably brings into conflict the requirements of industry and amenity and poses difficult problems of restoration.'

The 'barbaric mutilation' is there if you look, I don't doubt, but the first workings I found took me quite by surprise. From a ford near Moyles Court, well stocked with broadleaves and thirsty ponies, I took a road which wound back on itself as it bore me upward to a height I could not have imagined from the surrounding terrain, which had been irregular, but (I thought) without extremes.

Suddenly, I was in a lunar landscape among flying dust and deafening noise. I was there for just as long as it took the tyres to grip on the dead brown skin of the land and then, having added considerably to the airborne debris, I fled back downhill to the shady stream where ponies sipped on and children paddled.

Today, some of the private gravel workings which can be found on either side of the A338 between Ringwood and Fordingbridge have run out and the industrialists are laying upon them their own understanding of amenity, which pleases anglers and inland sailors but not always those who remember the spot before the pick and shovel moved in.

In fairness to the New Forest District Council, they have prepared a policy document relating to the Blashford/Ibsley area which seems to envisage best use of the options available. But it is still a matter for the test whether the recreational breakthrough which is filling up every crater and quarry in the Greater London area with water, fish, anglers and sails in that order will strike a chord in the heart of the grass-roots Forester, who only ever wanted the area to be as Nature intended.

The Forestry Commission attitude to sand, gravel and hoggin extraction is unequivocal. The 1971 consultative document, *Conservation of the New Forest*, a result of close liaison between Commission, Hampshire County Council, Nature Conservancy, New Forest Rural District Council (as it then was), Ringwood and Fordingbridge Rural District Council (ditto) and the Verderers states: 'We consider that . . . extraction on Crown Land should be limited to that required for use on that land and that planning permissions should not be granted for gravel extraction on private land within the perambulation.'

The up-dating *Statement of Future Strategy* (1978), says: 'The Review Group were of the opinion that the 1971 recommendations . . . be sustained.'

That theme runs through many of the other matters considered. The 1971 document was a good one and the phrase 'at present level' which persists in the 1978 version is in itself a compliment to the work and thought that went into its predecessor.

'At present level' for motor racing means a complete ban. Where it refers to orienteering, cycling, fishing, cricket, golf and football, model airctaft and boats, scenic drives, it means a block on extension to existing use.

The most recent strategy statement concludes in this way:

'The Review Group reiterate the concept that these proposals cannot be blueprints for the future but welcome the speed with which the Forestry Commission has implemented the original recommendations.

'The Group now see the Forest entering a period of consolidation and strengthening of the measures undertaken by the Forestry Commission. They do not envisage any major changes for the next few years but will, as a Group, assess success or failure of these conservation measures. This will ensure that steps can be taken in time, to further the protection of the traditional character of the New Forest.'

These are fine and comforting words – if only everybody can keep them in mind. From the outset, man has been not so much the fly in the ointment as the ointment which trapped the fly, and that must be true of these days when democracy decrees a multitude of voices and human nature ensures a multitude of views.

Most of the voices say they want what is best for the Forest – but most of them add that they alone know what that best should be. Whether they base their views on expertise or custom and practice, the result is a narrowing down of motive, a division of sympathy, a kiss of death.

A full consensus would take more pages than we have used already. But all ideas, provided they are presented through the right foci (which are there in the existing machinery) have a certainty of consideration and a better-than-usual chance that their merits or otherwise will be recognised.

The Forestry Commission – though their system of communication (distinct from their information service, which is artistic as well as impeccable) is criticised and there must be a basis for complaint in the fact of the criticism itself – cannot ride roughshod (if Donn Small will pardon the expression) over residential feelings, and the days are gone when they might attempt to keep an unsavoury policy under wraps . . . David Stagg gave the chuckle to that when he went to Alice Holt and blithely took all the notes he needed on the programme about which Dallas Mithen had been so guarded.

Not that I believe the present F.C. staff at Lyndhurst would brook any embargo of this nature – they are as impatient of the 'us-and-them' tag as any other quarter. To me, they have been more than helpful, abundantly forthcoming, undoubtedly honest.

The Nature Conservancy Council are also responsible to the Ministry of Agriculture but it would be a dangerous generalisation to suggest that they and the Commission are both servants of the same master. Messrs Tubbs and Small have a healthy respect for each other. They have certain tacit agreements about exchange of information and notice of intent. There is no guarantee that these same arrangements would prevail if one or both positions changed hands because the matrix is as informal as that. Their departments share a car park. I would not put the link any higher.

At the same time, let it not be thought that sanity rests on the friendship of two men. Whoever they were, there would still be binding constitutional considerations.

Under the 1973 Mandate, the Forestry Commission carry a responsibility for preservation as well as profit. Under an inter-departmental agreement, the Nature Conservancy Council has the power to veto any F.C. venture which might jeopardise the ecology.

The Verderers have all the teeth they need to operate control and restraint upon Forest developments – although the legislation which so empowers them could be less ambiguous.

Their present composition of five appointees and five electees may not suit all tastes but it would be difficult to conceive a different set-up which would not sway them towards either extremism or bureaucracy.

The argument I have heard time and again from various other sources has been, 'How can they hope to administer when they cannot even agree among themselves?' Such a complaint is more responsible for the contentions that persist than is the condition it cites. Administration without discussion – animated, at times – is dictatorship . . . and the real malaise (to give it a stature it neither warrants nor deserves) is that so many units would just love the chance to play the dictator. It is partisanship which directs most of the brickbats.

Of all interested parties, perhaps the Commoners are the ones who have changed least over 900 years and more. Whatever they did in the days of Canute was to safeguard their living and whatever they do now has the same objective. If they still jump as though they have been stung at most of the suggestions from elsewhere, put it down to race memory. History has not done them many favours.

Studied as a community, they reveal motivations closer to love than money and such rebellion as exists among individuals may well be a product more of generation than conviction.

Their dogmatic stance on all matters relating to grazing shows how close many of them live to the breadline. The dealer and the mercenary type are not unknown amongst them and personalities clash in that particular arena as they do in any place where two or three are gathered.

But one important factor should never be overlooked. If money were the prime consideration, many of them could best secure it by placing a 'For Sale' sign somewhere on their holdings, cashing in on the first 'good life' townsman who came along (and believe me, the urban rustics are queuing up) and buying a little spread of their own in Wales or the West Country where they didn't have to worry about marking fees, pannage months or burning quotas.

Yet they don't.

And the fact that they don't bespeaks a dedication to this area and a concern for its long-term welfare which should earn them places at any conference table . . . places pretty close to the head.

Other active lobbies – New Forest Pony Breeding and Cattle Society,

Hampshire Field Society New Forest Section, New Forest Association – are powered by the same vigour which activates the prime movers in the groups already mentioned.

That is an analysis of all the cases and it will be seen that the gulfs are not unscaleable if one tribe will speak peace with another.

Such a conversation is vital because these troubled waters need bridges and not poured oil . . . Which brings us to the latest threat.

All the trappings of a Texas oilfield, albeit on a miniature scale, already exist at Wytch in the north-east corner of the Purbeck peninsula; and the developer's arguments that his activities are too small to have any lasting effect, that beauty will be replaced, that the working is short-term, that in fact Britain needs this commodity for economic stability, have been exercised. I find no comfort in them.

Poole Harbour Commissioners have made their own quantification, which some call apocalyptic. If there is a spill of major proportions from the Arne field, they say, then it would take 50 or 60 years for the harbour area to recover – or less, depending on degree, or more, depending on what you mean by 'recover' . . . or even much more, depending on how much weight you give to unforeseeables.

Dorset County Council and representatives of smaller local councils have met Gas Council experts for an outlining of aspirations and safeguards. No matter how councillors feel – and few have been converted by the exercise in frankness – all they can do, one suspects, is to dig in their heels, or at least to drag their feet, along the road to inevitability.

And in the meantime, Purbeck makes its choice from holes for clay working, holes for subterranean water, holes for the carbon-gas mixture that hints at oil, bangs from vibreosis (which is the Gas Council's new way of monitoring the underlying layers) and bangs from the gunnery ranges which close some of the finest cliff walks around the British coastline for much of the year.

Purbeck is a different story and it would be misleading even to suggest that the New Forest is approaching a Wytch situation. However . . . Forestry Commission Deputy Surveyor Donn Small admits quite candidly that a New Forest oilfield would not (necessarily) be ruled out of hand.

'They don't all look like Texas now, with derricks everywhere,' he says. 'Just a little pumping engine here and there.

'And we would insist that pipes would have to be underground. After all, there are gas pipes underground already and the Forest is on the National Grid and nobody could say honestly that this has interefered with enjoyment.

'Besides, people have been drilling holes around here for 20 years and one would think they would have come up with something by now if it was there . . .'

Anthony Pasmore as a Verderer would insist that not only pipes but pumping houses should be underground – but he points out that he speaks as an individual and not as any kind of spokesman for the Swainmote.

He agrees that exploration has been going on for some time in the Forest, but with nothing like the impetus attained in the past two or three years. Perhaps the levels beneath Forest soil will prove unviable and the area will be spared first-strike manifestations.

But there is an alternative even more chilling.

British Petroleum and Gulf are so confident about pockets which exist under the sea off the Hants and Dorset coasts that they have indulged in major monitoring operations. Gulf, representing several concerns, use the phrase 'group shoot' to cover their function.

And if oil should be discovered in sufficient quantities beneath the Solent or Poole Harbour or Kimmeridge Bay, then it will have to come ashore somewhere. This being so, the more probable implication for the Forest would be in a second-strike capacity.

Already, on the eastern edge of the trees – at Fawley, on the Waterside – one of the largest refineries in the world is situated.

It has not always been an ideal neighbour. In March 1977, a small fire triggered a blow-out which rained oil droplets on Waterside villages. Esso's efforts to make amends – 2,700 homes visited, 75 cars washed, etc. – were spectacular and commendable. But residents would have been happier if the need had not arisen. And in 1978, it was left for the National Farmers' Union to announce that some 90 faults had been discovered in the pipeline from Fawley to West London, that some farmland had been affected by leakage and that compensation would be paid.

B.P. were quick to announce that nothing like this could happen to any of their admittedly shorter pipelines criss-crossing the Arne neck of the Purbeck peninsula.

Here is an object lesson. Prior to B.P. and Gulf marine activities, their most vociferous critics were the inshore fishermen, concerned about their lobsters and their pots.

The oil companies – at two meetings within four days – offered compensation in the event of damage, loss of earnings in the case of time spent moving pots out of the explorer's way . . . and the opposition just faded away.

The production of a cheque book and a suitably rounded figure might persuade inland individuals, too. But money is the cheap way out of it.

An assurance that accidents just don't happen with any regularity leaves me unconvinced. In a totally new situation, there is no way of telling when or how the first 'spill' could occur. And once that has happened, it will be useless to state that the chances are now ten million to one against repetition. One good accident would be quite enough to ruin everything.

New Forest M.P., Mr Patrick McNair-Wilson, has kept up a barrage of questions to the Energy Minister or his representative in an effort to obtain some clear statement on Government intentions on inland oil, but the response to date (mid-1978) has been platitudinous, either because a golden egg needs to be handled with extreme care or because the questioner was a member of Her Majesty's Opposition or both.

Local voters, Verderers, Commission have the power to control the situation locally and it is no good to say 'Maybe . . . We are keeping an eye on it . . . We will act when it happens.'

The answer should be ready now. And it should be 'KEEP OUT'.

And if the many facets of the New Forest personality cannot forget their differences to make that the verdict of them all, then we are down to hope . . . hope that, somewhere, waiting for his moment, is another William the Conqueror.

Epilogue

I could have left the Forest with threat weighing down every bough, but that is not the way of it. If old Ytene knows the hazard, he is not deterred; more concerned with keeping his inhabitants spellbound and holding his place under the rolling Hampshire sky.

The trees do the missionary work; the moorland is the evangelist. It is the gentlest and most relentless of conversions. Very soon, you know why you must fight to save this unique compendium of moods and visions – because faith is nothing without good works.

W.H. Hudson found a location which registered exactly the kind of existence beyond the bounds of time which he had felt and countless others before and since have known. Seated atop a burial mound on Beaulieu Heath, he could picture all these souls revivified and relaxed at the end of the day, their brown faces reddened by the dropping sun.

We also have a place where, paradoxically, the division of daylight and darkness only serves to underline the unbroken stream from yesterday and before to tomorrow and beyond. It faces west, as did Hudson's vantage point and it, too, hints at eternity among the reminders of the long-dead.

We found it in the orange period of a clear winter day. We had climbed between ferns, gorse and grass still sugared by the frost and found a pond transformed into a china plate by the regular overnight touches of ice, and had then turned to the view.

The terrain between Burley Street and Kingston has so many hummocks of such regular shapes that the whisper exists – I have heard it often but never been able to confirm it – that here, when Castle Hill was an Iron Age fort, lay a battlefield. If so, the battles must have been regular and steeped in casualties. The Ordnance Survey admits to only one discovered barrow, on Cranes Moor, slightly to the south.

It is easy enough to imagine all sorts of altercations as the locals set out from the fort to waylay unwary travellers moving inland from the great port of Hengistbury.

It was easy enough to imagine all manner of matters on our visit.

The whole area of Cranes Moor, Vales Moor and all the way up Verely Hill to Picket Post carries a network of paths . . . and a name: Smugglers Road. The sky was going from orange to red, the moorland from green to a powdery blue as it rolled away to the horizon. On the paths, figures moved, made vague and silhouettish, fuzzed at the edges by the sharpening light.

At just such a dusk, perhaps, the wayfarers had quickened their pace to be rid of the Forest by nightfall. At just such a dusk, more recently, silent men with pack-horses or donkeys had stepped out southward, skirting Bransgore and Hinton and coming finally to the bunnies of Chewton and Hordle where they could take illicit delivery of spirits and French silk once the moon waited on the water to be raked.

And then returned, struggling and cursing at the gradient, the pack-animals, the anxieties of their profession; keeping the hills between themselves and the emerging new day; watching for the signal swirl of Lovey Warne's scarlet petticoat.

Such comings and goings over this Forest ridgeway and all of them visible, with a little licence, a little abandonment of the usual co-ordinates. For it is not fanciful to ignore the limitations which today tries to set upon us. Rather, the reverse is true. Anybody who hopes to see all of the Forest by coin or clock or compass does himself a disservice.

Far better that he should take a lesson from the leaf. Through its chloroplasts, it absorbs not time and space but light and energy and all the necessities of its existence.

And in the New Forest, as nowhere else on earth, man can do the same.

Peace in the Forest – the gentlest and most relentless of conversions.

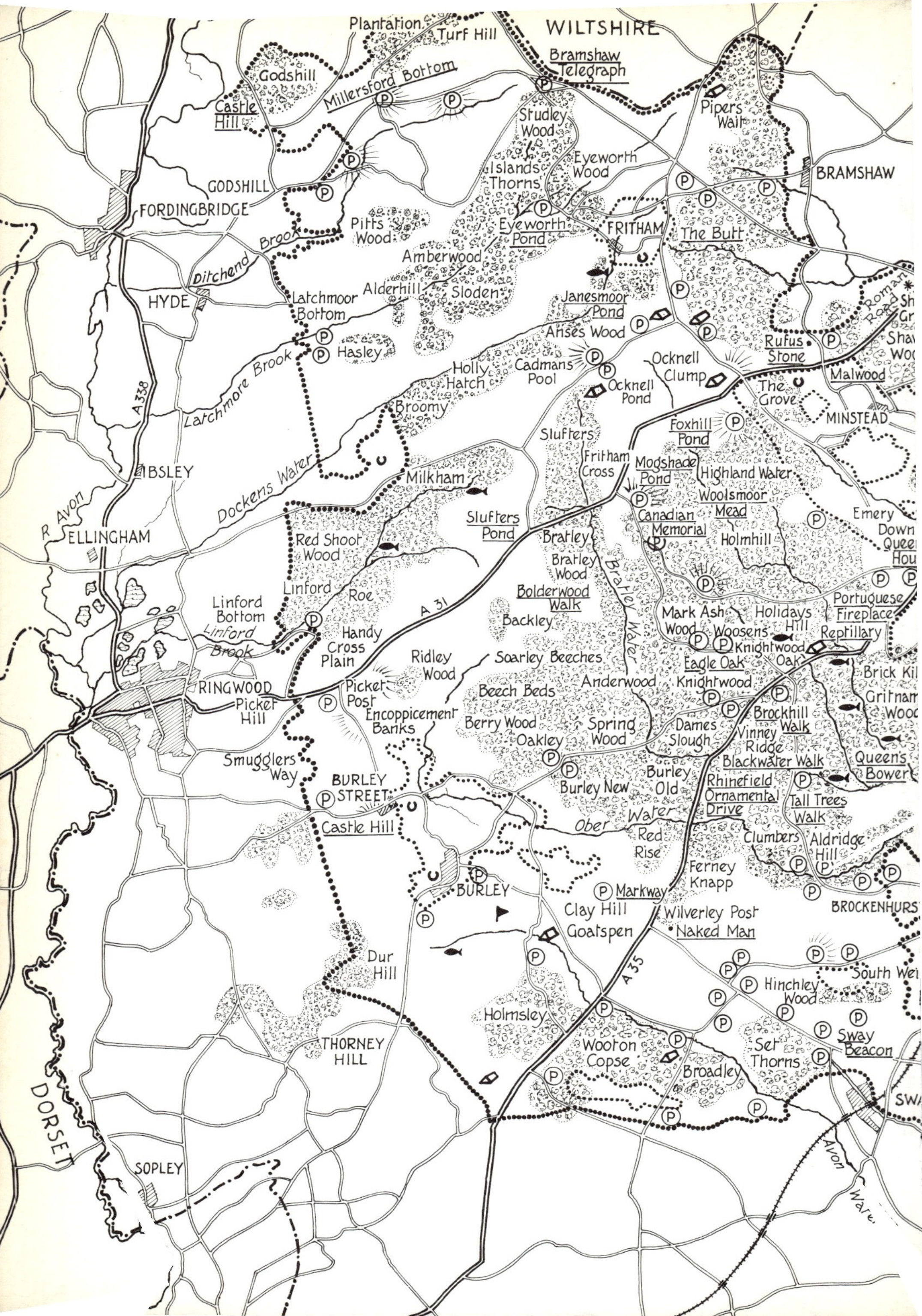

WILTSHIRE
Plantation
Turf Hill
Bramshaw Telegraph
Godshill
Millersford Bottom
Castle Hill
Studley Wood
Pipers Wait
Islands Thorns
Eyeworth Wood
GODSHILL
BRAMSHAW
FORDINGBRIDGE
Pitts Wood
Eyeworth Pond
FRITHAM
The Butt
Ditchend Brook
Amberwood
Alderhill
Sloden
HYDE
Latchmoor Bottom
Janesmoor Pond
Roman Road
Anses Wood
Hasley
Rufus Stone
Holly Hatch
Cadmans Pool
Ocknell Clump
Latchmore Brook
Ocknell Pond
Malwood
The Grove
Broomy
MINSTEAD
A338
Foxhill Pond
Slufters
Fritham Cross
Mogshade Pond
Highland Water
IBSLEY
Milkham
Dockens Water
Woolsmoor Mead
R Avon
Slufters Pond
Canadian Memorial
ELLINGHAM
Red Shoot Wood
Bratley
Holmhill
Emery Down
Bratley Wood
Bratley Water
Linford
Roe
Bolderwood Walk
Portuguese Fireplace
Linford Bottom
Backley
Mark Ash Wood
Holidays Hill
Linford Brook
Handy Cross Plain
A 31
Woosens
Reptillary
Ridley Wood
Soarley Beeches
Knightwood Oak
Eagle Oak
RINGWOOD
Picket Post
Picket Hill
Anderwood
Knightwood
Beech Beds
Encoppicement Banks
Berry Wood
Spring Wood
Dames Slough
Brockhill Walk
Oakley
Vinney Ridge
Smugglers Way
Blackwater Walk
Queen's Bower
BURLEY STREET
Burley New
Burley Old
Rhinefield Ornamental Drive
Tall Trees Walk
Castle Hill
Ober Water
Red Rise
Clumbers
Aldridge Hill
Ferney Knapp
BURLEY
Markway
BROCKENHURST
Clay Hill
Wilverley Post
Goatspen
Naked Man
Dur Hill
A35
South Weirs
Hinchley Wood
Holmsley
Sway Beacon
Wooton Copse
Set Thorns
THORNEY HILL
Broadley
DORSET
Avon Water
SOPLEY